POWER CARVING TOOLS

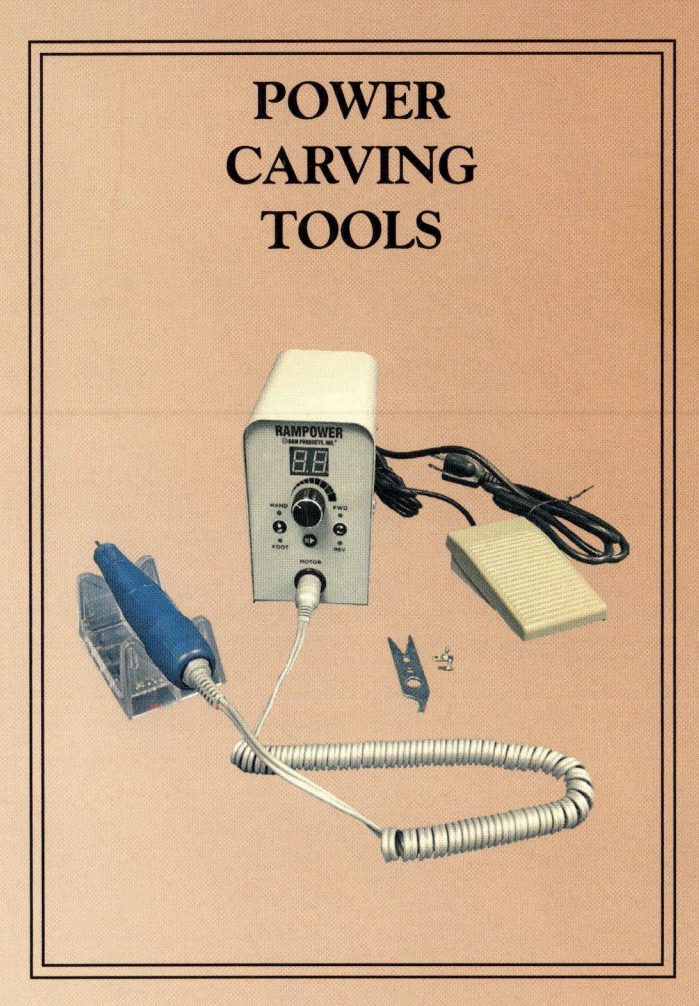

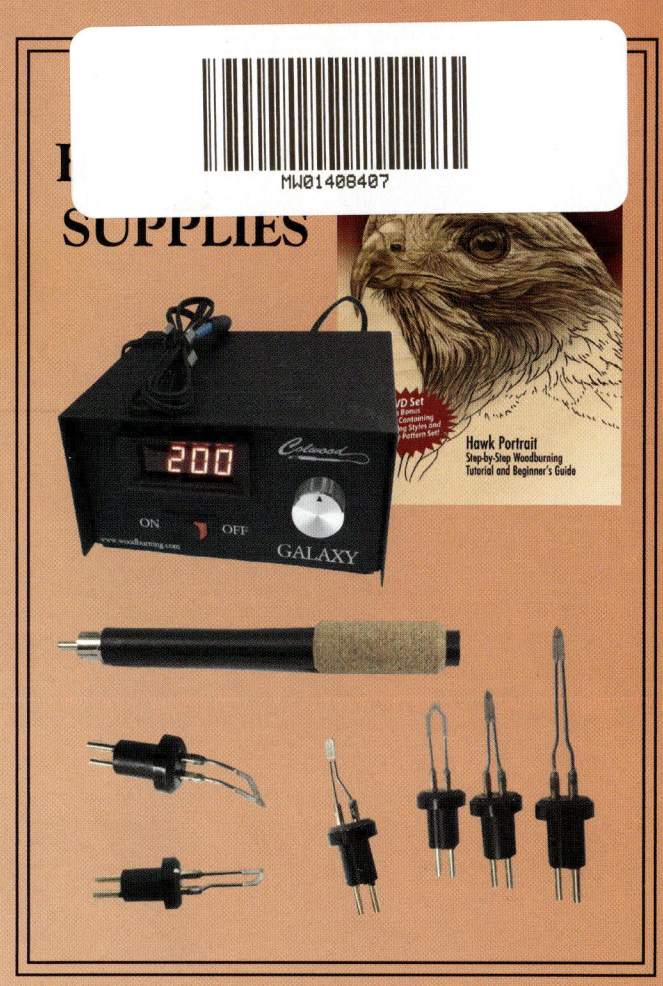

BURNING SUPPLIES

STUDY CASTS,

STUDY BILLS,

ROUGH OUTS,

CUT OUTS

BASSWOOD & TUPELO CARVING BLANKS

Wildfowl Carving MAGAZINE
THE BEST OF COMPETITION

Editor
Tom Huntington
Graphic Designer
Brittnee Longnecker
Advertising Director
Jenny Latwesen

BEST OF COMPETITION, A WILDFOWL CARVING MAGAZINE publication, is published by AMPRY PUBLISHING, LLC, 3400 Dundee Road, Suite 220, Northbrook, IL 60062. Contents copyright © 2018. All rights reserved. Reproduction in whole or in part without consent of the publisher is prohibited.

Canadian GST #R137954772

Advertising: (847) 513-6095
All correspondence should be addressed to:
The Best of Competition
P.O. Box 490
New Cumberland, PA 17070
(847) 513-6057
Fax: (847) 513-6099
www.wildfowl-carving.com

ISBN: 978-1-945550-33-1

Printed in the U.S.A.

FROM THE EDITOR

WILDFOWL CARVING'S GREATEST HITS

We've been publishing COMPETITION for 30 years now. Thirty years! There have been a lot of decoys under the bridge in those three decades, not to mention scores of songbirds, raptors, owls, shorebirds, and pretty much any other kind of feathered creature. There have been a lot of different shows, too. Some are still with us, and others are no more than fond memories.

WILDFOWL CARVING & COLLECTING MAGAZINE (as it was then called) explained how to make the birds, but COMPETITION was concerned with the finished products. The idea was to spotlight the best work from competitive carving shows across the country. Later the publication started covering some Canadian shows and eventually it ventured across the Atlantic to see what British carvers were doing. One thing we can deduce from the work we've featured over the years is that competition brings out the very best in carvers. When you're going against other top carvers, you push yourself a little bit more.

But it can be a two-edged sword. "The most valuable aspect of having competition such as this is the interest it creates in the art form, not only from artists or beginning artists, but from collectors and admirers of the art form as well," Pat Godin said at the 1990 Ward World Championship. "Unfortunately, to have a competition you must have rules which tend to restrict the artists. These rules force them to carve in a certain manner instead of carving whatever they want. But that's the nature of competition."

That is indeed the nature of competition, but sometimes being forced to work within limits can spark creativity. That may be the reason why the work you'll see within these pages is so astonishing. It's the work of bird carvers at the top of their games.

It wasn't easy picking the pieces that appear here. We wanted to show the best work while also casting the spotlight on as many different shows as we could. For every piece we selected, there were dozens of others that just wouldn't fit. The decisions about what to include and what to leave out were agonizing.

Looking through these pages, it's easy to feel a bit nostalgic about shows gone by. It's also easy to feel hopeful about the future of wildfowl carvings, because the quality of the work has not diminished over time. If anything, it just keeps getting better and better. The carvers from previous years were great, but so are the carvers of today, and so will be the carvers of tomorrow. I've enjoyed this look back at COMPETITIONS past, but I'm also looking forward to COMPETITIONS that are yet to come. Stay tuned!

Tom Huntington

ON THE COVER (clockwise from top left): *robin by Peter Kaune; blue-winged teal by Ashley Gray; Cooper's hawk by Pat Godin; sanderlings by Larry Barth.*

31st Anniversary

www.decoyguild.com

CORE SOUND DECOY FESTIVAL
December 1-2, 2018, Harkers Island, NC

SAVE $18 on Wildfowl Carving Magazine!

- 4 annual issues
- Stunning inspiration
- Carving tutorials
- Painting tips
- Expert techniques

SAVE 47%

Call toll-free to order at
(877) 762 - 8034 (U.S.)
(866) 375 - 7257 (Canada)
or visit www.Wildfowl-Carving.com/WMBOC18

Does your club or organization have a Wildfowl or Fish Carving related competition and show? If so we'd love to have you as an affiliate member.

JOIN THE IWCA AFFILIATES TODAY!

Your show doesn't have to be big, to be a BIG part of the IWCA. The benefits outweigh the annual membership fee of $250 and include:

- Current set of standardized rules for both Wildfowl and Fish Divisions.
- IWCA membership mailing list.
- A Show Rep position and voice on the IWCA Board of Directors.
- World-wide advertising in Wildfowl Carving Magazine.
- IWCA website promotion including a webpage promoting your event, posting of show results and show photos.
- Opportunities to host IWCA Championship events, including various awards.
- Opportunites to apply for Educational Grants and Seminars.

Grow Your Event As An IWCA Affiliate!
Contact IWCA Membership - Monty Willis
willisdecoys@gmail.com (252)-222-0492

30th Anniversary!

Congratulations, Wildfowl Carving Magazine!

On 30 Years of *Competition* Coverage. Well Done!
We are proud to have grown with you!

THE NEW P80 by Razertip®

AVAILABLE SEPTEMBER 1, 2018

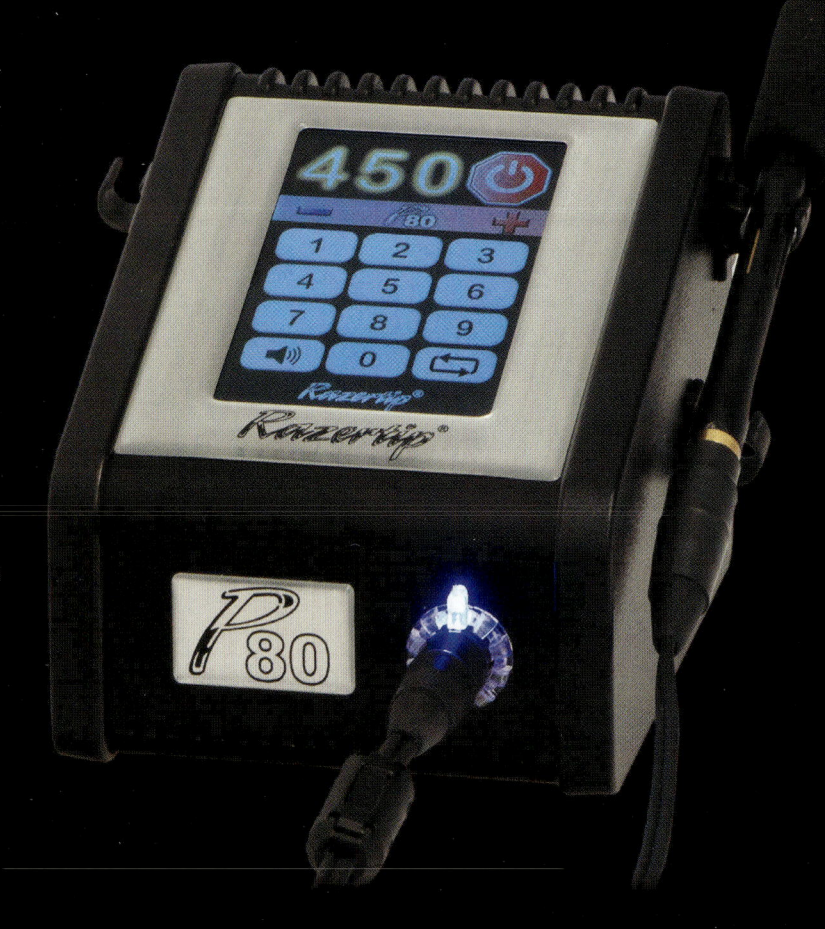

- UNIVERSAL POWER SUPPLY WORKS WORLDWIDE AND IS COMPLETELY UNAFFECTED BY VOLTAGE FLUCTUATIONS.

- COMPATIBLE WITH EXISTING RAZERTIP® PENS AND ACCESSORIES

- CAN BE EASILY CONVERTED TO DOUBLE OR TRIPLE UNIT WITH AVAILABLE EXPANSION MODULES

razertip.com/P80.htm

THE RESULT OF OVER 30 YEARS OF EXPERIENCE AND LISTENING TO CUSTOMER FEEDBACK

Razertip®

...Firing imagination since 1984...

Fine Pyrographic Tools & Portable Dust Collectors

Razertip Industries Inc.
- PO Box 910, 301- 9th Street North, Martensville, SK Canada S0K 2T0
- Phone 306-931-0889
- Toll-free order line 1-877-729-3787
- Email: info@razertip.com
- More information & free catalogue at razertip.com

WELCOME
TO THE BEST OF
COMPETITION

Wildfowl Carving & Collecting Magazine published its debut issue in the spring of 1985. It wasn't long before the magazine's publishers saw a niche they could fill. Competitions were popular events in the carving community, and it seemed natural to create an annual publication that would spotlight the winning entries at various shows.

"From my vantage point as the editor of Wildfowl Carving & Collecting Magazine, I see a very dynamic art form, one that changes and grows, in part, because of competitions," wrote Cathy Hart in her note at the start of Competition 1988, our first annual showcase.

Competition is still going strong 30 years later. That milestone prompted us to open our files and highlight some of the amazing work we've covered over the decades. And it truly is amazing work. We hope you enjoy this trip down memory lane—a lane strewn with wood chips, sawdust, and paint splatters.

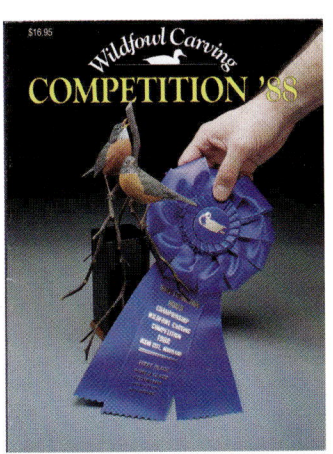

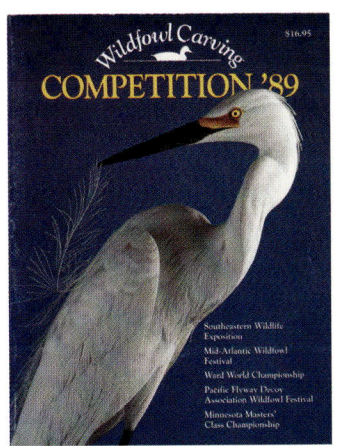

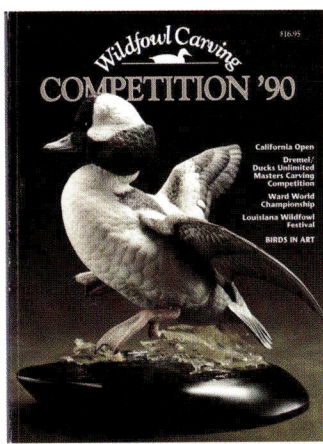

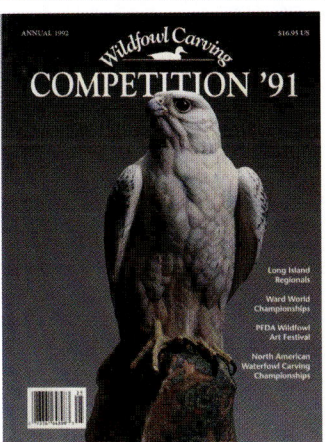

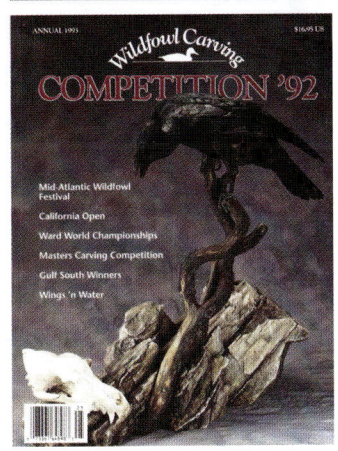

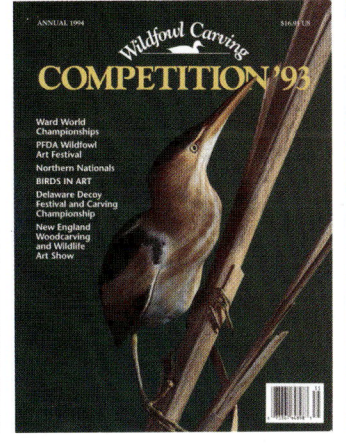

Carvers Profiled in Competition

Vanessa Adams • Dave and Mary Ahrendt • Michael Arthurs • Tom Baldwin • Jerry Barkley • Larry Barth • Roger Barton • Paul Beaulieu • Alan Bell • Bob Berry • Rick Bobincheck • Chris Bonner • Weldon Bordelon • Lynn Branson • Don Brewer • Ed Brown • William Browne III • Jett Brunet • Jude Brunet • Gary Joe Bryan • Dan Burgette • James F. Carlisle, Sr. • Jerry and Bev Carson • Andy Chlupsa • Tom Christie • Mark Christopher • Andrea Cooke • Luke Costilow

WWW.WILDFOWL-CARVING.COM

• Mark Costilow • Lana Cowell • Jack Cox • Carl Danos • Gary De Cew • Fausto Del Grosso • Anthony Donato • Kent Duff • Steve Durkee • Lionel Dwyer • Lonnie Dye • Gary Eigenberger • Bunny Farley • Lawrence Fell • Richard Finch • Mike Ford • Al Forler • Tim Forler • Paul Foytack, Jr. • Jack Franco • Al Fulford • Phil Galatas • Lee Garbel • Walter Gaskill • Martin Gates • Maria Gay • John Gewerth • Gerry Glaves • Pat Godin • Ashley Gray • Pat Grebeck • Bob Guge • Bob Hand, Jr. • Carol Happley • Michael Harde • Gordon Hare • Jim Hazeley • Del Herbert • Thomas Horn • Yasuko Iida • David Inglefield • Forrest "Bud" Jennings • Rick Johannsen • Jon Jones • Al Jordan • Eric Kaiser • Norm Kanieski • Peter Kaune • William Kennedy • Vic Kirkman • Thomas Kraemer • Jeff Krete • Robert Kroese • Sina "Pat" Kurman • Ron Lace • Glenn Ladenberger • Bob Lavender • John Leeder • Chalres (Duke) Leeper • Bruce Lepper • Larry Livingston • Laura Lucio • June Lyon • Frank MacFarlane • Richard F. Magane • Van Keuren Marshall • Russell Martin, Jr. • Gary Mascara • Doug Mason • Robbie Matherne • Thoms Matus • Peter McClaren

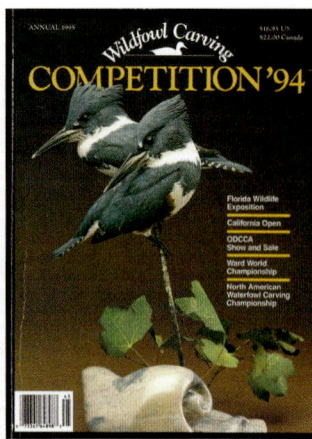

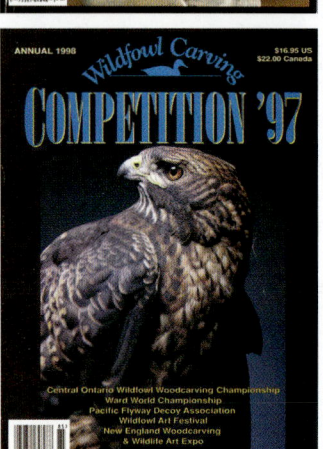

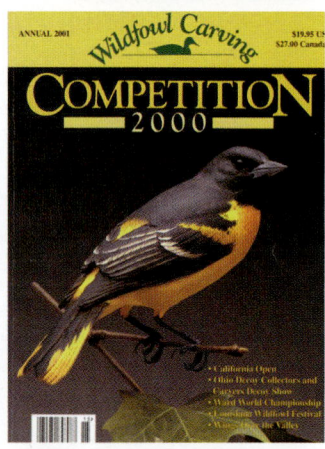

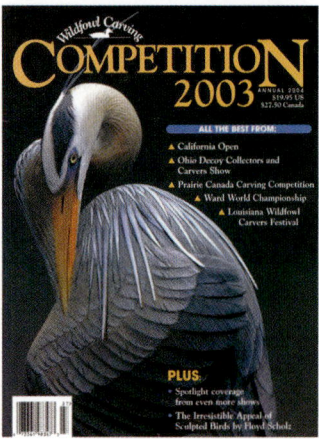

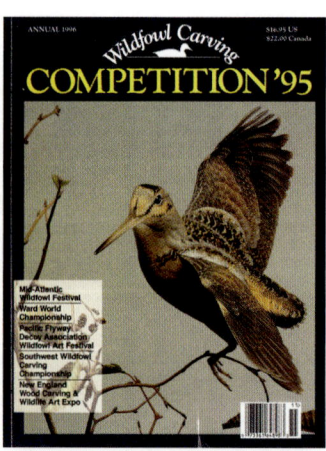

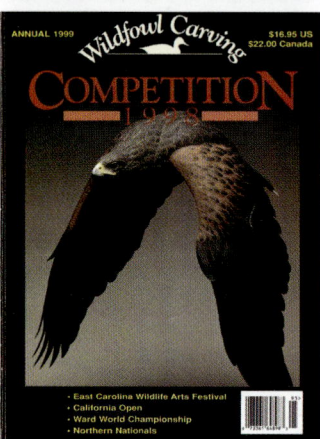

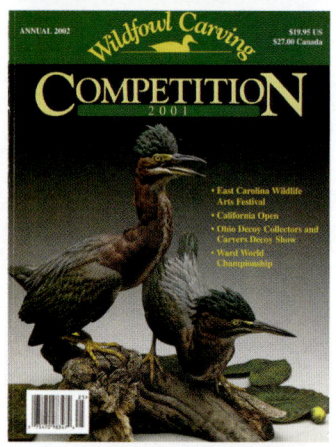

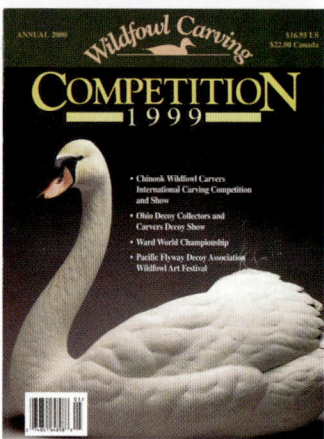

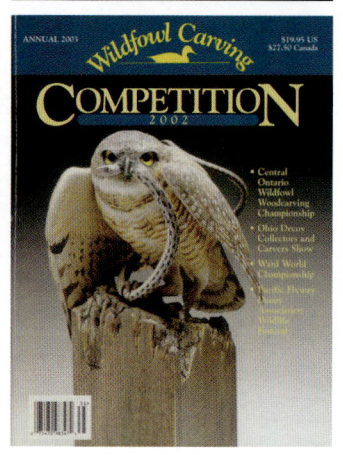

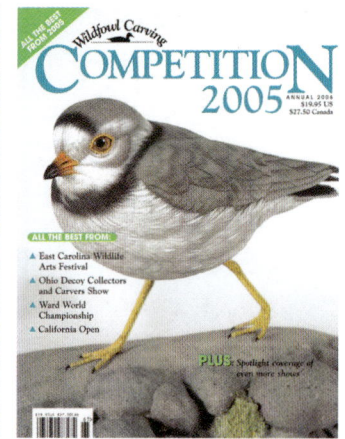

BEST OF COMPETITION

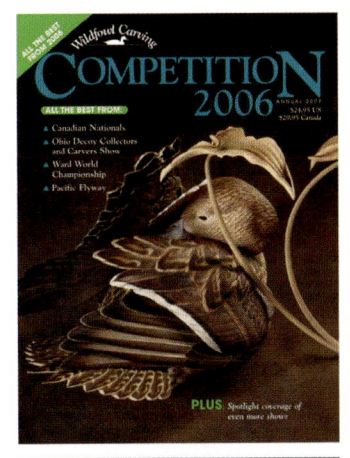

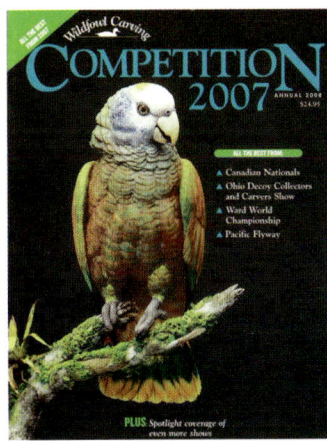

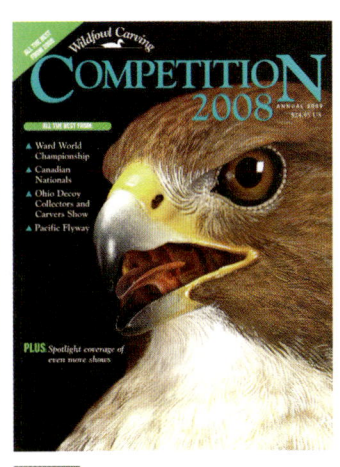

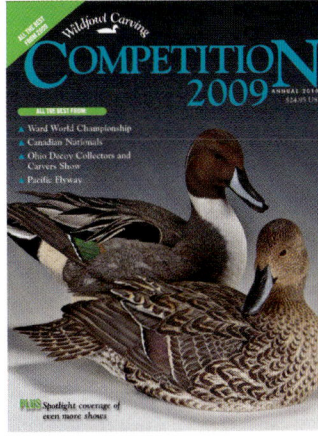

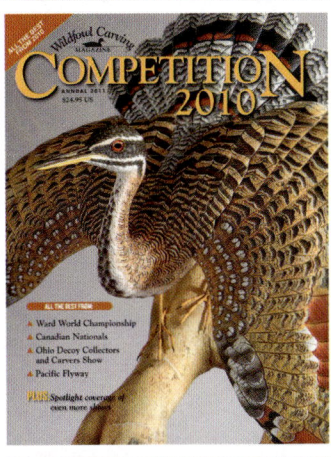

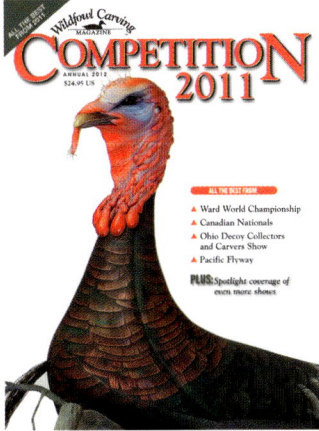

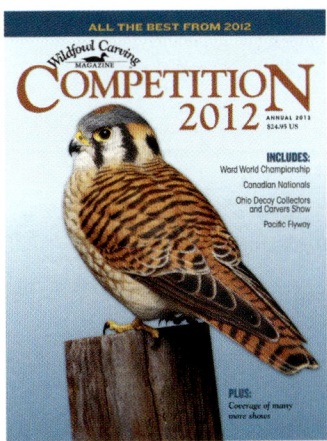

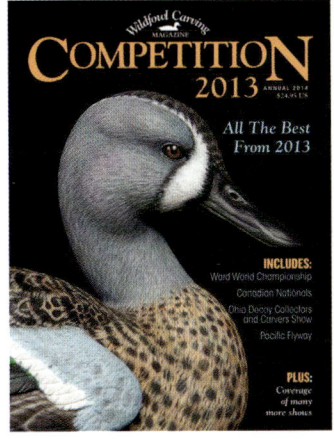

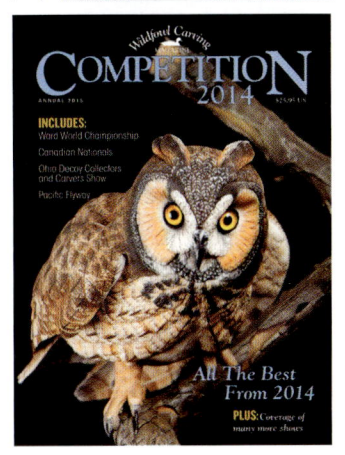

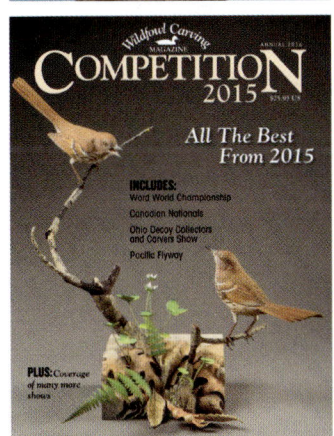

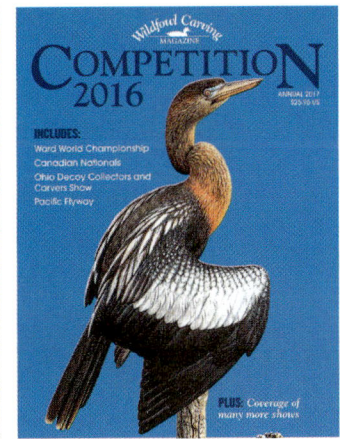

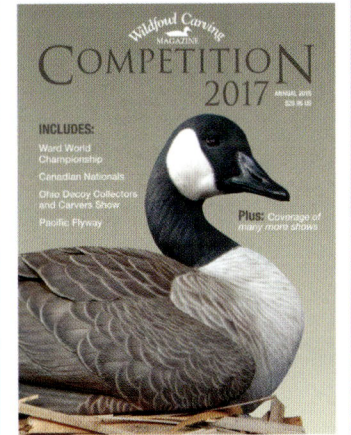

• Laura McIntosh • Glenn McMurdo • Jean Minaudier • Ray Minaudier • Dale Mogielka • Daniel Montano • Keith Mueller • Jeff Muhs • Fred Negrijn • James Neidigh • Michael Nesbit • Bill Nitzsche • Leo and Lee Osborne • Leo Osborne • Richard Otsubo • Bill Palmer • Peter Palumbo • Tom Park • Victor Paroyan • Greg Pedersen • Tom Pellis • Don Phalen • Chau Pham • Dennis Poeschel • Charlie Prinz • Gilles Prud'Homme • Lia Rahm • Jeff Rechin • Richard Reeves • Dick Rhode • Tommy Rogers • Lenoard Rousseau • Rusty Rutherford • John Scallen • Floyd Scholz • Marcus Schultz • Dennis Schroeder • John Sharp • Jerry Simchuk • Wayne Simkin • Mark Slatcoff • Theodore Smith • Ross Smoker • Matt Sneebold • Judy Snyder • Carol Speegle • Michael Stewart • Tommy Stewart • Mark Strucko • Thomas Stuck • Ken Stuparyk • Jerry Talton • Greg and Judy Taylor • Ted Trusz • Larry Vanderhyde • Jimmie Vizier • Norm Walsh • Martin H. Ward • Harvey Welch • Jamie Welsh • George Wickham • Dan Williams • R.D. Wilson • Todd Wohlt • Greg Woodard • Gary Yoder • Joe Zalik • Peter Zaluzec

WWW.WILDFOWL-CARVING.COM

COMPETITION 1988

"What you're reading right now, the premier edition of COMPETITION, celebrates the exciting arena of competitive bird carving with informative feature stories and highlights of last year's contests in breathtaking color photographs."

So wrote editor Cathy Hart in her introduction to COMPETITION 1988. This first edition was actually rather modest in its coverage, including only four competitions and one exhibition. Two of the competitions, the Ward World Championship and the Louisiana Wildfowl Festival, are still in business 30 years later. Another show, the California Open, closed its doors after its 2017 show, and the North American Wildfowl Carving Championship in Livonia, Michigan, ended years ago. The one exhibition featured in the issue, the Masters' Show in Ligonier, Pennsylvania, is another one for the history books.

The debut edition of COMPETITION also featured a photo essay on the late, great John Scheeler, as well as articles about competition in general, and results listings.

DRAKE BLUE-WINGED TEAL
by Pat Godin

JOHN SOBCZAK

Best in Show, Decorative Floating, at 1988's North American Wildfowl Carving Championship.

The robins accepting the blue ribbon on the cover were carved by Peter Kaune. They won Best in World Decorative Miniature Wildfowl at the 1988 Ward World Championship. Dan Williams took the photo.

FLYCATCHERS
by Lonnie Dye

Best in Gulf South, Decorative Life-size Wildfowl, at the 1988 Louisiana Wildfowl Festival. Dye used welded steel rod for the branches and epoxy putty for the bark. The leaves were paper, attached with fishing line.

BILL A. WARNER

BEST OF COMPETITION

1988

DRAKE MALLARD
by Jett Brunet

JOHN SOBCZAK

Best of Show at the 1988 North American Wildfowl Carving Championship.

KESTREL
by Gordon Hare

DAN WILLIAMS

Best in World Decorative Life-size Wildfowl at the 1988 Ward World Championship. It was the second time Hare won this division.

In Their Own Words

"The fierce dignity of this little bird impressed me. What I first noticed was that this bird is always moving and very much interested in its environment. The pose had to reflect this agitation somehow, but not in an overly obvious way."

WWW.WILDFOWL-CARVING.COM

CANADA GOOSE
by Richard Reeves

Best of Show, Competition-grade Decorative Decoys, at the 1988 Louisiana show.

BILL A. WARNER

MERLIN
by Greg Woodard

Best of Show, Decorative Life-size, Open, at the 1988 California Open.

DAN WILLIAMS

BEST OF COMPETITION

Want to add books like these to your shelf?

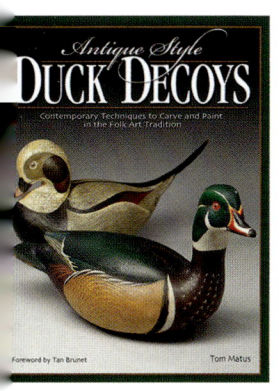

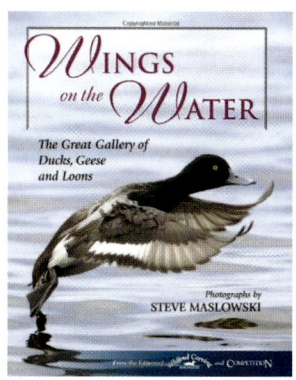

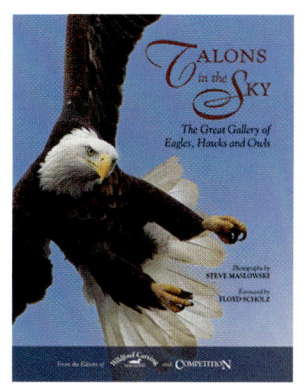

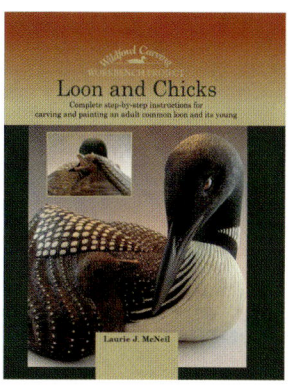

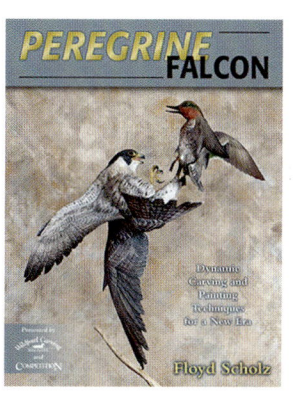

Join the *Wildfowl Carving* Magazine Book Club! It's easy as 1-2-3!

1 Join the *Wildfowl Carving* Book Club and receive our latest release hot off the press! Becoming a member is 100% FREE, and you can cancel your membership at any time.
Call us toll-free to join the book club at (877) 762 - 8034
Canadian customers call (866) 375 - 7257
Give PROMO Code: **WBCSU18**
Or join the book club online at www.WildfowlCarvingMagazineService.com/bookclub

2 After we process your membership, we will send you our latest book.

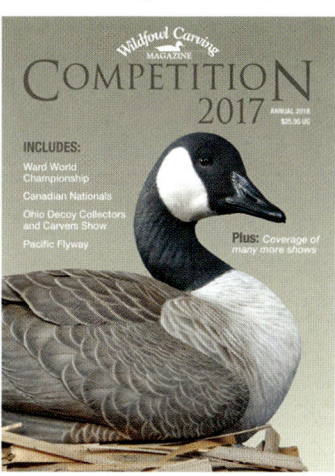

Pssst!

See the finest carvings from the year's top shows with this annual installment. Carvers and collectors will marvel at the award-winning carvings of ducks, raptors, songbirds, and more!

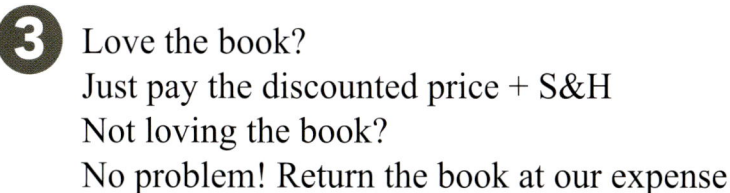

3 Love the book?
Just pay the discounted price + S&H
Not loving the book?
No problem! Return the book at our expense

WBCSU18

FREE Previews. GUARANTEED Discounts. FREE Book Returns.

COMPETITION 1989

ROBINS
by Gary Yoder

Best in World Decorative Life-size Wildfowl at the 1989 Ward World Championship. The win also earned Yoder the $20,000 John Scheeler Memorial Award.

DAN WILLIAMS

In Their Own Words

"I was not going to enter this piece, but five minutes before getting into the car to come to Ocean City, my brother told me I should bring it along. No one was more surprised than I when my name was announced as the winner! This piece started about four years ago but didn't come together until this past winter when I developed a severe case of cabin fever."

The second edition of COMPETITION offered quite a different lineup from the debut issue. The only show returning from COMPETITION 1988 was the Ward World Championship, but several new shows filled out the coverage. One of those was the Southeastern Wildlife Exposition in Charleston, South Carolina. Technically it was an exhibition, not a competition, but the show did include a small carving competition. Robert Hortman of Mt. Holly, South Carolina, won best of show with a woodcock.

The show coverage even extended overseas for a look at the European Decoy Carving Championship. "There is something slightly unsettling about walking into an auditorium in an English village and seeing tables lined with wildfowl carvings, duck decoys, carving supplies, and paints," wrote correspondent Curtis J. Badger. "The scene is so typically American that you feel as though you've been swept away in some sort of Jules Verne time machine to Ocean City, or New Orleans, or Livonia."

The Pacific Flyway Decoy Association's show, still featured in COMPETITION to date, and the Minnesota Masters' Class Championship rounded out the coverage. COMPETITION 1989 also featured the first appearances by a number of noted carvers, including Rich Smoker, Gary Yoder, Kent Duff, and Floyd Scholz (whose snowy egret graced the cover).

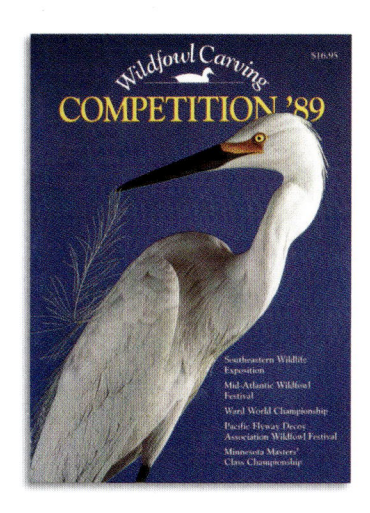

Floyd Scholz carved the life-size snowy egret on the cover, which won first place at the Minnesota Masters' Championship. Scott Jacobson took the picture.

PEREGRINE FALCON
by Phil Galatas

DAN WILLIAMS

Best in World Decorative Miniature Wildfowl at the 1989 Ward World Championship.

In Their Own Words

"I have a great admiration for birds of prey. One of my favorites is the peregrine falcon. It exhibits a lot of speed and agility in the air. But it also shows speed as it is perched, and its very bearing puts forth intelligence. This impresses me. But instead of putting him in flight, I wanted to capture the moment right before flight."

In Their Own Words

"The goals I set really make me dedicate myself to my art in order to reach them. I established a goal to be a World Champion like my father, and another to repeat the accomplishment. After achieving these goals, I needed something a bit different and maybe even more out of reach. So I set a goal for myself to sweep this division because it's never been done before. No one has ever taken first, second, and third in any division and this was what I needed to motivate myself. I decided to enter four birds, but I ran out of time and only had three birds to enter. Because of this, I couldn't afford to have any bird falter."

HEN GADWALL
by Jett Brunet

Third in Decorative Life-size Floating Waterfowl, Open, at the 1989 Ward World Championship. Brunet swept the division, with a redhead drake taking first and a pintail drake second.

DAN WILLIAMS

BEST OF COMPETITION

1989

SWALLOWS
by Jim Hazeley

Best of Show, Life-size Decoratives, Open, at the 1989 Mid-Atlantic Wildfowl Festival in Virginia Beach.

DAN WILLIAMS

BEST OF COMPETITION

1989

MERGANSERS
by Chris Bonner

Best in World Decorative Life-size Waterfowl Pairs at the 1989 Ward show.

DAN WILLIAMS

In Their Own Words

"Developing the attitude of the subjects is what I consider to be one of my strongest and most enjoyable tasks.... The base does nothing for the pair of birds as they sit on the water. All you have is your birds. The shape is everything, and that's why I put so much emphasis into shape."

COMPETITION 1990

COMPETITION 1990 continued to expand the coverage of the competitive world by adding shows to the publication's lineup. The new arrivals included the California Open in San Diego and the Birds in Art juried exhibition at the Leigh Yawkey Woodson Art Museum in Wausau, Wisconsin. These two shows continued to appear in COMPETITION for years to come. Other shows that were new to COMPETITION's pages were the second annual Dremel/Ducks Unlimited Masters Carving Competition, which took place in Racine, Wisconsin, and the Chinook Carvers Competition in Calgary, Alberta. It also featured work by carvers who would become familiar names, among them Larry Barth and Bob Guge.

In an article called "The Inside Story," Don McKinlay provided a primer on what to expect when entering birds into competition. "Taking the first step and deciding to enter a competition is a hard one," he wrote. "In the end, though, competitions are well worth facing the intimidation."

SHOVELERS
by Dennis Schroeder

Best in World Floating Decorative Life-size Waterfowl Pairs at the 1990 Ward World Championship.

DAN WILLIAMS

RED-BILLED TROPICBIRD
by Larry Barth

Second, Decorative Miniature Wildfowl, Open, at the 1990 Ward World Championship.

DAN WILLIAMS

The bufflehead on the cover was carved by Bob Perrish of Livonia, Michigan. It won best of show at the Dremel/Ducks Unlimited Masters Carving Championship. The photo was by Bela Horvath of Horvath Studios in Milwaukee.

HERON
by Gary Yoder

Best of Show, Decorative Miniature Wildfowl, Open, at the 1990 Ward show.

DAN WILLIAMS

In Their Own Words

"This particular piece was completed as a 50th wedding anniversary present and was not done specifically for competition. It was not a piece where I allowed myself a lot of time to second-guess my work. It was influenced by a tri-colored heron done by John Scheeler about four or five years ago which was kind of a breakthrough piece. He got involved in color combination and techniques such as wet-on-wet painting and thin and thick areas of paint where you could actually see the brushstrokes on the bird."

RED-TAILED HAWK
by Phil Galatas

Best in World Decorative Miniature Wildfowl at the 1990 Ward show. Galatas called the piece *Highland Defender*.

DAN WILLIAMS

In Their Own Words

"I chose the red-tailed hawk because it is a flying machine. Not necessarily for speed, but because it soars for such long periods of time. It has broad, powerful wings, big talons, and can handle larger prey. It's a very intense bird. I can never recall seeing a red tail that appeared to be relaxed."

1990

In Their Own Words

"This piece evolved from what was to be a preening black duck. I made a clay model and really didn't like it at all. It seems that the 1990s call for more than just a simple, nicely carved, burned, and textured decoy. I changed the model into a charging black duck because I wanted more animation. Even with the water there wasn't enough motion, so I added the grebe and had the black duck going after it. From observation, I realized that the black duck is very territorial and this was a natural thing for it to do."

BLACK DUCK AND GREBE
by Todd Wohlt

Best in World Decorative Life-size Wildfowl at the 1990 Ward show. At 21, Wohlt became the youngest carver to win a best in world title.

DAN WILLIAMS

In Their Own Words

"My desire to do this piece came from the love I have for this bird. The red-breasted merganser is such an incredibly dynamic species with a great subtle color scheme. The hen is actually part of a pair and was designed as such. It's not just one decoy. I did not enter the drake because I don't enter more than one decoy of the same species in a class. I guess that's because the best the other bird could possibly do is second place, and I don't want them competing against each other."

HEN MERGANSER
by Pat Godin

First, Decorative Life-size Floating Waterfowl, Open, at the 1990 Ward show. Godin made the crest feathers from PVC strips shaved down very thin and then frayed.

DAN WILLIAMS

COMPETITION 1991

With the early editions of COMPETITION, it seems like the only constant was change. Well, not really. There had been some consistency, too. For instance, the 1991 edition retained coverage of the Ward World Championship and the Pacific Flyway show, but it also added the Long Island Regional Carving Competition and the North American Wildfowl Carving Championship. The Long Island show took place in a castle, the former home of Howard Gould (son of financier and railroad magnate Jay Gould).

Another new feature, "Future World Winners," put the spotlight on winners at the novice and intermediate level. "Many of today's best artists began their carving careers at the novice level and worked their way up the ladder of success," noted the editors.

Another element of consistency was the high quality of the carvings within its pages. If anything, the pieces just got better and better.

MERLIN
by Bob Hand

First, Birds of Prey, and Best in Show, Decorative Life-size Wildfowl, at the 1991 Long Island Regional Carving Competition.

ROGER SCHROEDER

Greg Woodard carved the gyrfalcon on the cover. It won first in birds of prey at the 1991 Pacific Flyway Decoy Association Wildfowl Festival. It also finished second in the Decorative Life-size competition. Patrick Barreto took the photo.

CARDINAL
by Bob Guge

Best in World Decorative Miniature Wildfowl at the 1991 Ward World Championship.

DANA WILLIAMS

In Their Own Words

"As usual, I was working until the last minute on the piece, including painting in the hotel room. I didn't think the piece would win but was very pleased with it and was hopeful it might place. When my name was announced for first place, it was the biggest shock I've ever had in competition. But I don't mind a shock if it comes with a check!"

LONG-TAILED DUCKS
by Dennis Schroeder

Best in World Floating Decorative Life-size Pairs at the 1991 Ward show.

In Their Own Words

"Both the male and female oldsquaw are carved from a single block of tupelo wood, with the exception of the tail on the drake. I use power tools in the initial roughing out stages, then switch to knives and chisels to finish the carving process. The birds are then painted with oils."

DAN WILLIAMS

TURNSTONE
by Peter Palumbo

First in Class, Shorebird Division B, at the Long Island show in 1991.

ROGER SCHROEDER

BEST OF COMPETITION

1991

DRAKE PINTAIL
by Pat Godin

DAN WILLIAMS

Best of Show, Decorative Life-size Floating, at the 1991 Pacific Flyway show. It also won Best of Show at the North American competition.

LOGGERHEAD SHRIKE
by Larry Barth

DAN WILLIAMS

Best in World Decorative Life-size Wildfowl at the 1991 Ward show. Barth titled the piece *Vantage Point*.

In Their Own Words

"In Vantage Point, *I dealt with the bird, a loggerhead shrike, in my usual manner. But with the habitat—in this case a hawthorn branch—rather than duplicate it, I chose to artistically represent it. I decided that sharp, jagged, bare metal would be an ideal material to represent sharp, jagged hawthorn. I enjoyed the integration between my subject matter, material, and techniques. To me, the brass branch says 'hawthorn' and conveys something of the plant's character more effectively than if I had textured and painted it exactly like a real branch."*

WWW.WILDFOWL-CARVING.COM

COMPETITION 1992

"Art Wing" was a new section introduced in COMPETITION 1992. This "news journal of today's wildfowl sculpture" aimed to keep readers updated about developments in the carving world. It remained a regular feature of COMPETITION for the next two editions. Show coverage continued to expand in the 1992 edition. In addition to the Ward Show, the California Open and Birds in Art, it included the Mid-Atlantic Wildfowl Festival in Virginia Beach, the final outing of the Masters Carving Competition in Racine, Wisconsin, the Wings 'n Water Festival on the New Jersey shore, and the return of the Louisiana Show.

One of the carvers profiled in this issue was Tom Christie, who won the IWCA National Hunting Decoy Championship and the Ward show's Shootin' Stool contest in 1992. "I learn something new every time I make a decoy and every time I attend a competition," he said.

BLUE-WINGED TEAL
by Ashley Gray

Best of Show at the 1992 Wings 'n' Water Festival. Gray, who was only 20, carved the birds from a single block of tupelo.

DAN WILLIAMS

Todd Wohlt carved the crow on the cover. It won the people's choice award at the Masters Carving Competition in 1992, and second best of show in Decorative Life-size at the Mid-Atlantic Wildfowl Festival. Bela Horvath of Horvath Studios in Milwaukee took the photo.

RED-TAILED HAWK
by Floyd Scholz

Second Best in World Life-size Decorative Wildfowl at the 1992 Ward World Championship.

ROBIN
by Peter Kaune

Best of Show at the 1992 California Open.

WWW.WILDFOWL-CARVING.COM

29

KESTREL
by Greg Woodard

Best in World Decorative Life-size Wildfowl at the 1992 Ward World Championship. Woodard titled the piece *Cactus Flower*.

DAN WILLIAMS

In Their Own Words

"Typically, I try to keep my carvings all in one piece, but a cactus is so segmented that it seemed to make sense to make it in sections. I love cacti and the desert, and I wanted to put them all together. I kind of carved some flower buds on it, too, to go with the name."

BLUE-WINGED TEAL
by Victor Paroyan

Best in World Decorative Life-size Floating Pairs at the 1992 Ward show.

DAN WILLIAMS

In Their Own Words

"Last year's drake also had his mouth open, and I knew what I did wrong. I try to learn from my mistakes. In the end, the hen came out better. It was the first hen I ever carved."

30   BEST OF COMPETITION

1992

YELLOW RAILS
by Peter Zaluzec

DAN WILLIAMS

Best in World Decorative Miniature Wildfowl at the 1992 Ward World Championship. Zaluzec called the sculpture *Water's Edge*.

In Their Own Words

"I carried the image of that piece around in my head for a long time—the rails, the grasses, the precarious grip of their feet—until I just had to make it. . . . To get the anatomy where it should be, it's easier to use clay than wood. I can make a clay model in several hours."

COMPETITION 1993

When Curtis J. Badger wrote about the Ward World Championship in COMPETITION 1993, he mused how visiting Martians might have been baffled by the scene, as hundreds of humans at the show obsessed over the wooden birds while not seeming to care about the real gulls and sparrows flapping about outside. No doubt the alien visitors would have found it to be "curious behavior."

But there would have been no mystery for the people involved in the competitions covered this time out, which now included the Delaware Decoy Festival and Carving Championship in the town of Odessa, and the New England Woodcarving and Wildlife Show in Cromwell, Connecticut. Nor would it be a mystery for the people who continue to compete today and share their fascination with wooden birds.

BLUE-WINGED TEAL
by Ashley Gray

Best of Show, Floating Decoratives, at the 1993 New England Wood Carving and Wildlife Art Expo.

PATRICK BARRETO

In Their Own Words

"Finding new ideas and new concepts is difficult; but it makes me think, and perhaps gives me an edge.... I don't just take a block of wood and cut it out on a band saw; I spend a lot of time learning about particular species. I keep an aviary with a pond. I keep some birds for study and for my own enjoyment."

RUFFED GROUSE
by Pat Godin

Best of Show, Non-floating Decorative Life-size Wildfowl, National Level, at the 1993 Northern Nationals.

PATRICK BARRETO

Larry Barth carved the least bittern that appeared on the cover. The piece, which also included a marsh hen, won Best in World Decorative Life-size Wildfowl at the 1993 Ward World Championship. It was Barth's fourth world championship since 1985. Bob McGee of Lens Art in Salisbury, Maryland, took the photo.

PLATE-BILLED MOUNTAIN TOUCAN
by Peter Zaluzec

Best in World Decorative Miniature Wildfowl at the Ward show in 1993.

In Their Own Words

"I wanted to carve a non-North American bird, and I had seen a painting of a toucan that really impressed me. That provided the basis for building my work.... I couldn't find any reference photos, so I used the skins [study skins from the Chicago Field Museum] to get the correct measurements and colors. I read the field guides and studied the bird's environment, which I wanted to convey in the carving."

In Their Own Words

"I average four or five days to a bird. But, I usually don't do the whole bird in one shot. I carve until I'm tired of it or until I get the attitude and anatomy right. Then I may stop and put it aside. Finishing is the next step. To me, it means putting on the final touches, sanding, cleaning the carving up—making all the details sharp. When I feel like painting, I'll do that; it's the part I really like the best. I paint with oils because I believe them to be a premium art medium."

HEN SHOVELER
by Keith Mueller

Best in Show at the 1993 New England Wood Carving and Wildlife Art Expo.

BEST OF COMPETITION

1993

RING-NECKS
by Jude Brunet

DAN WILLIAMS

Best in World Floating Decorative Waterfowl Pairs at the 1993 Ward Show.

In Their Own Words

"I worked on texturing and painting in 1993. The ring-necks fit my painting style better than the blue-winged teal [the designated species in 1992], so I was more confident. I knew I had improved, and I spent a lot of time on the birds. I started in November when we got back from the Easton Waterfowl Festival, and really got serious after Christmas. I made only one other bird, a gunning decoy, between then and April."

HEN GREEN-WINGED TEAL
by Jett Brunet

PATRICK BARRETO

Best in Show, Decoratives, at the 1993 Pacific Flyway show.

In Their Own Words

"Anyone can learn how to burn and texture a bird, and I think too much emphasis sometimes is put on that. What the old carvers did was so appealing—the grace, the aesthetics, the lines that the Ward brothers and the Vizier family created decades ago.... The judges and the public may be getting more educated regarding these artistic qualities."

WWW.WILDFOWL-CARVING.COM

COMPETITION 1994

Competition 1994 added some new events to the lineup. In Florida, the Florida Wildlife Expo had its first show, held at the Omni Centroplex in Orlando on a January weekend of driving rain. Wildfowl Carving & Collecting Magazine sponsored the woodcarving competition. Also making its Competition debut was the Ohio Decoy Collectors and Carvers Association's annual show. The venue was the Holiday Inn in Westlake, Ohio. "The show caters to collectors of antique decoys as well as carvers and appreciators of contemporary works," noted correspondent Lisa Lujanac. Coverage of the ODCCA show, now held in Strongsville, continues in Competition today.

HEN PINTAIL
by Rick Johannsen

Best of Show, Floating Decorative Decoys Open, at the 1994 ODCCA show.

DAN WILLIAMS

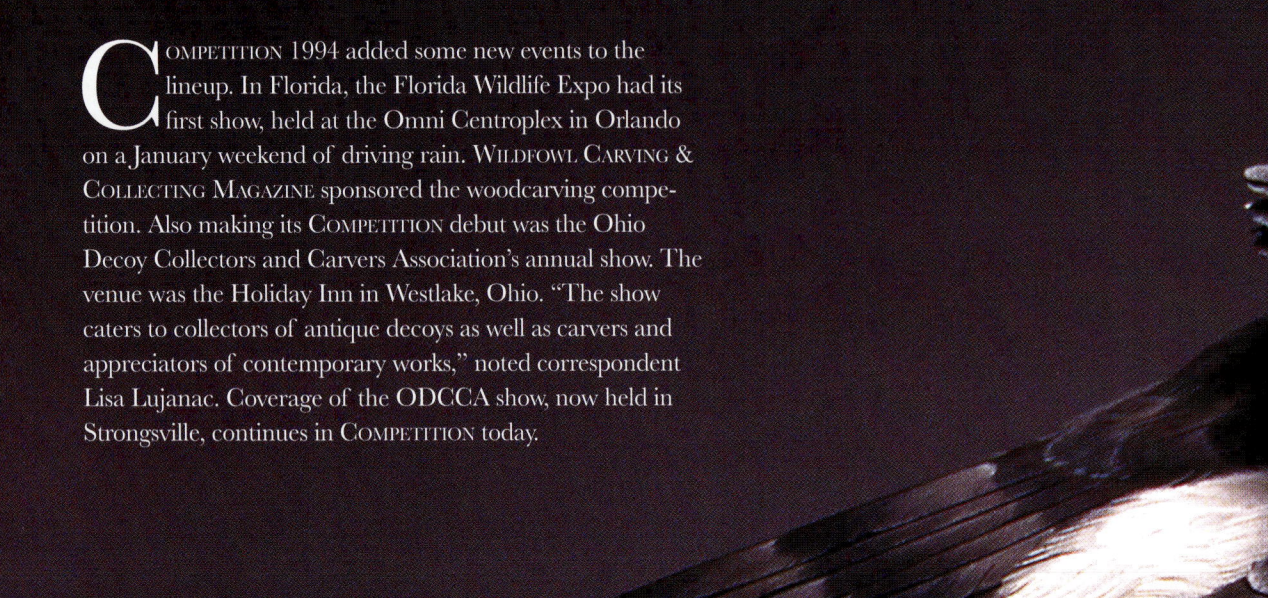

The belted kingfishers on the cover were carved by Mark Christopher of Oviedo, Florida. They won the O-Town Open Professional Best of Show Award at the first annual Florida Winter Nationals and were photographed by Randy Batista of Media Image Photography in Gainesville, Florida.

NORTHERN GOSHAWK
by Glenn Ladenberger

DAN WILLIAMS

Best in World Decorative Life-size Wildfowl at the 1994 Ward show.

In Their Own Words

"I had a really good feeling about this carving. Although this has definitely been my most difficult and challenging piece, I just felt that this one was going to be the winner. It was a great feeling to watch total strangers as they looked at my hawk before the judging and picked it as their selection to win. This year I came to the competition feeling like I had paid my dues and I really believed it was my year."

GREEN-BACKED HERON
by Todd Wohlt

Selected for the 1994 Birds in Art exhibition, and also Third in World Decorative Life-size Wildfowl at the Ward World Championship.

DAN WILLIAMS

EMPEROR GOOSE
by Jon Jones

Best in World Decorative Life-size Pairs at the 1994 Ward show.

DAN WILLIAMS

In Their Own Words

"Every feather has four or five colors. It took a lot more effort and time to paint the emperor than other birds I have done, but painting is my favorite part of the process. It is at the painting stage that the bird really starts to come to life."

BEST OF COMPETITION

1994

GOLDEN EAGLE
by Ashley Gray

New England Grand Champion at the 1994 New England show. Gray called the sculpture *Spirit Messenger*.

DRAKE GADWALL
by Jett Brunet

DAN WILLIAMS

Best in Decorative Life-size Floating Waterfowl, Open, at the 1994 Ward show.

COMPETITION 1995

GREAT EGRET
by Marcus Schultz

Best of Show at the 1995 North American Wildfowl Carving Championship.

MCDONALD PHOTOGRAPHIC DESIGN STUDIO

In Their Own Words

"It's an apparently simple-looking piece with some abstraction. The bird is gazing just beyond the perimeter of the base. Radiating rings appear to be emanating from the point of his gaze. The apparent movement of the rings, actually the 'flame grain' of the wood, cross the annual growth rings at right angles, suggesting an 'overlayment' of water activity. Rhythms of shape and line direction, the turn and thrust of the egret's neck, together with the array of the root network, fall in complementary, radiating directions."

A number of familiar names remained on the roster of the 1995 edition, including the Ward World Championship, the Mid-Atlantic Wildfowl Festival, and the Pacific Flyway. New this year was the Southwest Wildfowl Carving Championship, which took place in a town called Grapevine, just outside Dallas, Texas. Virginia Beach once again hosted the Mid-Atlantic show.

For several issues, COMPETITION had been highlighting upcoming young carvers in a section called "Future World Winners?" Jude Brunet was featured in 1991 and went on to fulfill the prediction. One of the carvers singled out in COMPETITION 1995 was Larry Fell, who won a best of show at the Ward's intermediate level for a scaup. In 2017, Fell went on to win a best in world title in the pairs division, with a white-fronted goose.

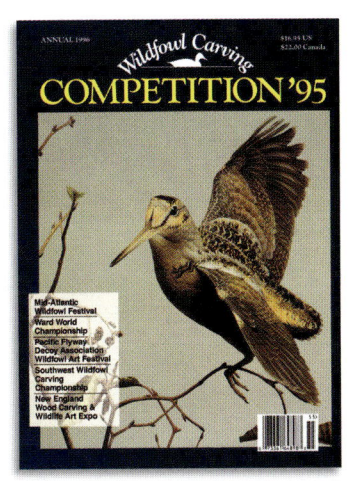

Pat Godin carved the American woodcock on the cover. He called the sculpture *Descent Through the Alders*. The piece won Best in World Decorative Life-size Wildfowl at the 1995 Ward show. Brian Barrer of Stroud, Ontario, took the photo.

ANHINGA by Jeff Muhs

Best in World Interpretive at the 1995 Ward World Championship. Muhs called the piece *Sun Worshipper*.

PEREGRINE FALCON by Ashley Gray

Best of Show at the 1995 New England competition.

WWW.WILDFOWL-CARVING.COM

SCREECH OWLS
by Richard Finch

Best of Show at the 1995 Southwest Wildfowl Carving Championship.

MCDONALD PHOTOGRAPHIC DESIGN STUDIO

In Their Own Words

"Including two birds gave me a chance to create a piece that wouldn't have a dead spot. I wanted something that would have interest on all sides. Since I had won the Gulf South Championship in 1989 with a life-size pair of gray-phased owls, I thought I'd change one to a red-phase. I have to admit, I like the gray-phase a little more than the red. There's more vermiculation, more subtle changes in color going on."

BEST OF COMPETITION

1995

RICHARDSON'S GOOSE
by Sina Kurman

Best of Show, Decorative Floating Waterfowl, at the 1995 Mid-Atlantic show.

In Their Own Words

"I was trying to find a more natural position in which to present her. Theoretically, she's building a nest. I wanted to show some animation to make her a little different. I like to try to assign some greater meaning to my carvings, to raise an eyebrow."

HEN MALLARD
by Maria Gay

Best of Show, Professional Decorative Floating, at the 1995 New England Expo.

COMPETITION 1996

The show lineup remained steady in 1996, and COMPETITION featured eight shows. As reported by editorial assistant (and future editor) Candice Tennant, the 1996 Ward World Championship persevered despite distractions from major ongoing renovations at the convention center in Ocean City, and a violent thunderstorm on Saturday. Tennant also reported from the Northern Nationals, enlivened when the carvers in the B.O.S.S. Championship, unable to pick a winner, let Marcus Schultz's puppy make the final decision.

The carver profiles this year offered a new wrinkle—photographs of the subjects. Now readers could identify the carvers they were reading about.

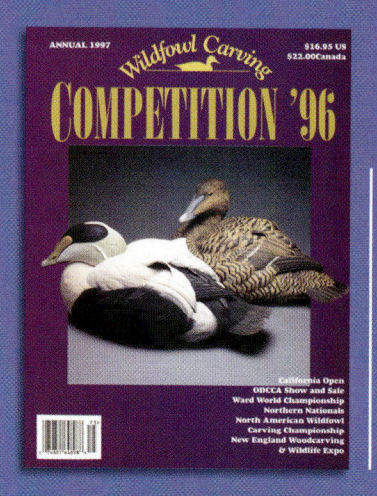

The eider pair on the cover is the work of Keith Mueller. He called them *Eager Indifference* and they won the World Pairs competition at the 1996 Ward World Championship. Dan Williams took the photo.

DOVE
by Ashley Gray

Best of Show at the New England Woodcarving and Wildlife Art Expo in 1996. Gray called the piece *The Spirit Carries On.*

GOLDEN PLOVER
by Marcus Schultz

Best of Show, Decorative Life-size Wildfowl, Open, at the 1996 Northern Nationals.

In Their Own Words

"I painted a lot of three-dimensional shapes into the feathers to infer that the light source is coming from above. Because the bird is banking, the highlights are on top of the feathers and the shadows are underneath.... I wanted the bird to be flying through the branches as opposed to flying beside them. To create this illusion, I placed the bird at a downward angle and positioned a branch over the top of the head."

COOPER'S HAWK
by Pat Godin

Best of Show, Standing Decoratives, at the 1996 North American Wildfowl Carving Championship.

SCOTT JACOBSON PHOTOGRAPHY

OWLS
by Lynn Branson

Best of Show, Interpretive Sculpture, and People's Choice at the 1996 California Open.

MICHAEL FRITZ

BEST OF COMPETITION

1996

KESTREL
by Todd Wohlt

Best in World Decorative Life-size Wildfowl at the 1996 Ward World Championship.

DAN WILLIAMS

In Their Own Words

"I wanted to make a competitive piece that was simple in design. The kestrel allowed me to do this in a successful manner. The blues and oranges complement each other nicely, and the bird's large head and small overall size also make it appealing."

WWW.WILDFOWL-CARVING.COM

COMPETITION 1997

It wasn't until COMPETITION 1997 that the publication finally strayed north of the American border and covered a Canadian show. The Central Ontario Wildfowl Woodcarving Championship, which took place in Kitchener, Ontario, later changed its name to the Canadian National Wildfowl Carving Championship and remains a part of COMPETITION's regular coverage. But that wasn't all the Canadian coverage: COMPETITION 1997 also included the Chinook Wildfowl Carving Competition and Show. Canadian carvers have always been among the art form's best talent, so it seemed about time COMPETITION included their shows.

DRAKE WIGEON
by Glenn McMurdo

Conestoga Rovers Purchase Award at the 1997 Central Ontario show.

ERNIE SPARKS

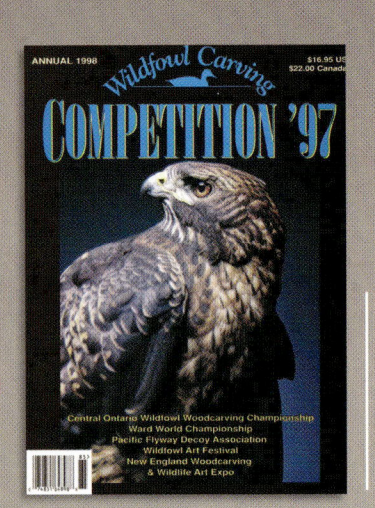

Greg Woodard carved the sculpture of a red-tailed hawk and kestrel that appeared on the cover. (This is a detail shot of the hawk.) He called the piece *Get Off My Cloud*. It won Best in World Decorative Lifesize Wildfowl at the 1997 World Championship. Dan Williams took the photo.

SORA RAIL
by Sina "Pat" Kurman

Best in Show, Decorative Life-size Waterfowl, at the 1997 Pacific Flyway Decoy Association show. Kurman called the piece *Across the Flats*.

MICHAEL FRITZ

In Their Own Words

"The biggest challenge was making the drake pintail's head. It is difficult to get the character out of it. It is also hard to create a realistic pattern on the drake's scapular feathers. I chose to keep both birds simple and just go for that graceful pintail character."

PINTAILS
by Victor Paroyan

Best in World Decorative Life-size Pairs at the 1997 Ward World Championship.

DAN WILLIAMS

BEST OF COMPETITION

1997

INDIGO BUNTING
by Todd Wohlt

Best of World Decorative Miniature Wildfowl at the 1997 Ward show.

DAN WILLIAMS

In Their Own Words

"Normally, I never burn in feather edges—to me it looks too harsh. The charred wood from using the side of the burner to define a feather edge 'ghosts' through the paint job. The feathers on the bunting, however, were so small that I had to do this. Knives weren't holding any detail. I set the burner low enough so that the ghosting didn't occur."

GREAT REED WARBLER
by Larry Barth

Best in World Decorative Life-size Wildfowl at the 1997 Ward show.

DAN WILLIAMS

In Their Own Words

"I went on a trip to Poland in 1992 with a group of artists and spent two weeks in a remote village on the edge of a marsh. On the last morning, I went out in a punt and saw many birds, but was struck by the sculptural power of the great reed warbler as it perched—perfectly balanced—on a long, thin reed. I sketched the bird on the spot, and it became one of several pieces that I was inspired to do by the trip."

COMPETITION 1998

The East Carolina Wildlife Arts Festival joined the COMPETITION lineup for the 1998 issue. The show in the North Carolina town of Washington had its third annual outing that year, and editor Cathy Hart said it had "the potential to become a regular stop on the carving show circuit." And it was, until the final show in 2016. Musing about the California Open's silver anniversary show, editor Cathy Hart wondered how a show survives for two decades. "A seasoned team with inspired leaders at the helm is certainly a key ingredient," she decided. And so was the show's feeling of hospitality. Apparently that was enough to keep that show going through 2017, but nothing lasts forever.

Glenn Ladenberger carved the Harris's hawk that appeared on the cover. Titled *Desert Reign*, the hawk won Best in World Decorative Life-size Wildfowl at the 1998 Ward World Championship. Ernie Sparks took the photograph.

HEN WIGEON
by Pat Godin

Winner of the Grand Master's Championship at the 1998 Northern Nationals. Godin called this *Wigeon and Watercress*.

ERNIE SPARKS

In Their Own Words

"The simplicity of the design can be deceptive. It is a great advantage, even with simple pieces, to work out the design on paper or, preferably, with a three-dimensional clay model. The model performs the same function as a two-dimensional sketch for a painting on canvas. A slight turn or twist of the head can sometimes make the difference in capturing the desired attitude. A design in clay will tell you quickly what will work."

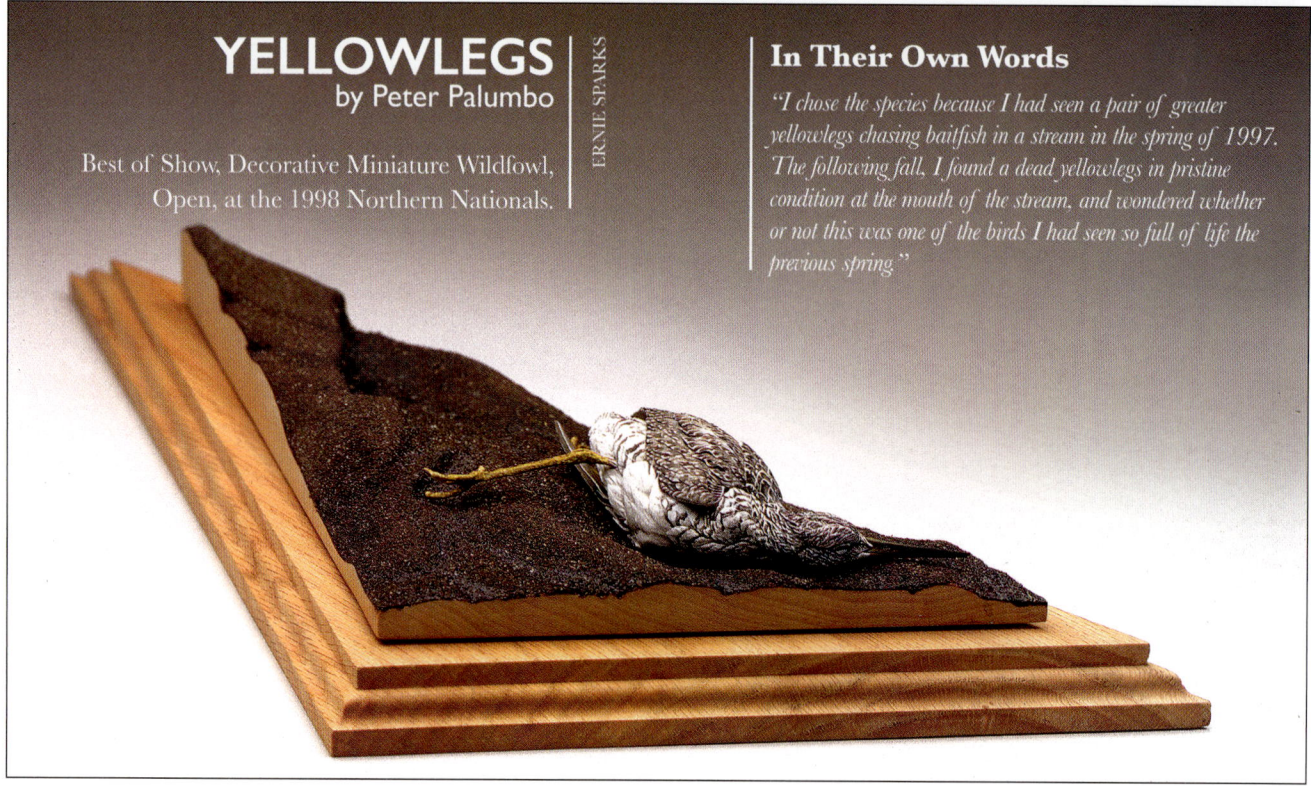

In Their Own Words

"There is more going on in the carving than what is seen from this photo angle. Running through the puddle are four different tread designs angularly crossing and dividing it into four separate sections of water. It was difficult getting the flatness of the water in and around the tread patterns. I have also carved a disturbance in the water's surface in the form of concentric rings caused by the birds' drinking, thus adding the circular aspect of geometry."

DOVES
by John T. Sharp

ERNIE SPARKS

Best in World Interpretive at the 1998 Ward World Championship. He titled this piece *Muddy Road*.

YELLOWLEGS
by Peter Palumbo

ERNIE SPARKS

Best of Show, Decorative Miniature Wildfowl, Open, at the 1998 Northern Nationals.

In Their Own Words

"I chose the species because I had seen a pair of greater yellowlegs chasing baitfish in a stream in the spring of 1997. The following fall, I found a dead yellowlegs in pristine condition at the mouth of the stream, and wondered whether or not this was one of the birds I had seen so full of life the previous spring."

54   BEST OF COMPETITION

1998

PENGUINS
by Jeff Rechin

ERNIE SPARKS

Best in World Miniature Decorative Wildfowl at the 1998 Ward World Championship. This was Rechin's first entry at the world level.

In Their Own Words

"With the penguins, the most difficult part was getting down between the birds because of how tightly they're grouped together. I made an extension to my knife blade because there was no room for any part of the knife handle between them. It may seem that it would have been easier to use a power tool to get between the birds, but power tools tend to 'fuzz' basswood, and I wanted a nice, flat surface."

WILLET
by Jimmy Vizier

BOB CERESA

Best of Show, Service Class Shorebirds, at the 1998 Northern Nationals.

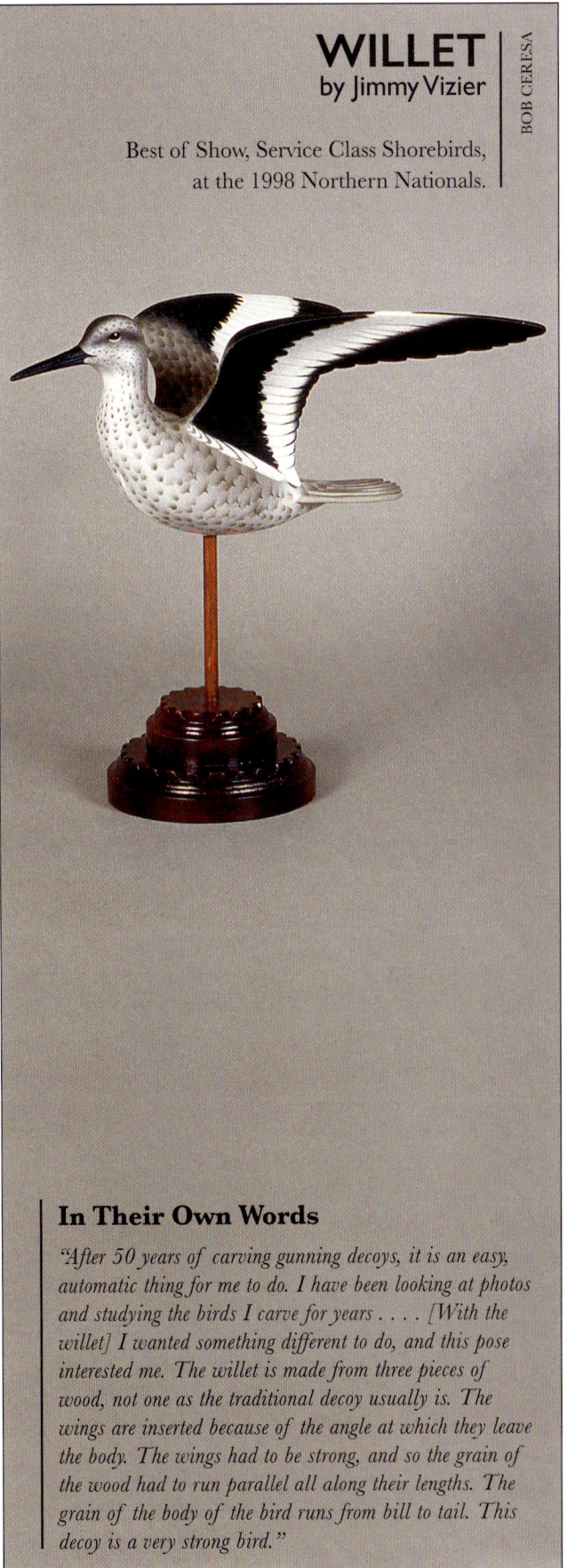

In Their Own Words

"After 50 years of carving gunning decoys, it is an easy, automatic thing for me to do. I have been looking at photos and studying the birds I carve for years.... [With the willet] I wanted something different to do, and this pose interested me. The willet is made from three pieces of wood, not one as the traditional decoy usually is. The wings are inserted because of the angle at which they leave the body. The wings had to be strong, and so the grain of the wood had to run parallel all along their lengths. The grain of the body of the bird runs from bill to tail. This decoy is a very strong bird."

COMPETITION 1999

GREEN HERON
by Larry Barth

Best in World Decorative Life-size Wildfowl at the 1999 Ward World Championship.

ERNIE SPARKS

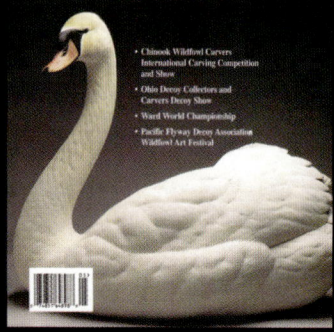

The goose on the cover is the work of Russell Martin, Jr. He called it *Grace*, and the carving won Best in World Decorative Life-size Waterfowl at the 1999 Ward World Championship. Ernie Sparks took the photo.

In Their Own Words

"I wanted to involve the space around the piece, as much or more than the space the piece actually takes up. A base gives a bird confines, and focuses attention where the artist wants it focused. I wanted to draw attention to the beauty of the bird. Without a base, the green heron claims the entire surface it is on, and the viewer's attention is completely on the bird."

In her write-up about the 1999 Ward World Championship, assistant editor Candice Tennant listed some questions that still get asked at shows today. "How did that artist take a subject that has been seen at so many shows before and make it completely new?" was one. Another was, "Why don't we see more of that species in competition?" And the third—probably the most common query since the beginning of wildfowl carving—was "How'd they do that?"

COMPETITION 1999 included coverage of the usual shows, plus some quick looks at work from the Chesapeake Challenge, the North Carolina Decoy Championship, and the New England Grand Championship. And you can bet that at some point people at all these shows just had to ask, "How'd they do that?"

LEAST TERN
by Del Herbert

Best in Show, Wildfowl as Sculpture, at the 1999 Pacific Flyway.

RICHARD MELNE, JR.

HEN BLACK DUCK
by Dennis Schroeder

Best of Show, Decorative Life-size Floating Waterfowl, Open, at the 1999 Pacific Flyway Decoy Association Wildlife Art Festival.

RICHARD MELNE, JR.

WWW.WILDFOWL-CARVING.COM

57

TRUMPETER SWAN CYGNET
by Karen Lesch

Winner of the $20,000 Purchase Award at the 1999 Northern Nationals.

ERNIE SPARKS

BEST OF COMPETITION

1999

GROUSE
by Pat Godin

In Their Own Words

"The tendency with life-size is to show only the necessary elements of habitat. With a miniature, I could include more habitat without overwhelming the piece. I had never done a miniature composition before, so the scaling down and composition of the piece were a challenge. The design elements were different, but the work itself was very similar."

Best in World Decorative Miniature Wildfowl at the 1999 Ward show. This was Godin's sixth Best in World title and his first in miniatures.

ERNIE SPARKS

HEN PINTAIL
by Rick Johannsen

Best of Show, Hunting Decoys, Open, at the 1999 Ohio Decoy Collectors and Carvers Association show.

ERNIE SPARKS

COMPETITION 2000

Remember the Y2K panic? According to some experts, a computer glitch would cause worldwide havoc as 1999 transformed into 2000. It didn't happen, and COMPETITION 2000 and the shows it covered survived just fine. There were some new events in the 2000 edition, including the Brant Festival in Parksville, British Columbia, on beautiful Vancouver Island. The show has had some venue changes since, but it remains part of the COMPETITION lineup. Not so with Wings over the Valley, hosted in Fallon, Nevada, for the second year. It was the show's only appearance in COMPETITION. And, for the second time, COMPETITION ventured overseas, this time to cover the National Wildlife Carving Exhibition in Norfolk, England, and its "selection of the best of British bird carving."

TURKEYS
by Jeff Rechin

ERNIE SPARKS

Best in World Miniature Decorative Wildfowl at the 2000 Ward World Championship. This was Rechin's second world title in miniatures.

In Their Own Words

"It took several subtle changes to get the piece to look as simple and natural as I could. I needed to position the birds so they would maintain a natural eye contact, and so that their action would visually stand out to the viewer. Clay models played a huge role in achieving this end."

MANDARINS
by Richard Otsubo

Best of Show, Open Decorative Life-size, at the 2000 California Open.

RICHARD MELINE, JR.

Bruce Lepper carved the oriole on the cover. It won Best in Masters Decorative Miniature Wildfowl at the 2000 Ward World Championship. Ernie Sparks took the photo.

SUNBITTERN
by Marcus Schultz

Best of Show, Masters Decorative Life-size Wildfowl, at the 2000 Ward World Championship. The sunbittern also won top honors in Rest of the Marsh at the ODCCA show that year.

ERNIE SPARKS

RED-BREASTED MERGANSERS
by Tom Matus

Best in World Shootin' Rig at the 2000 Ward World Championship.

ERNIE SPARKS

In Their Own Words

"I actually made five birds and chose the best three. Then I floated the birds and it was very difficult to get a good pose without the birds rolling a lot. The pre-dive drake was truly difficult to float. I found that it was going to need more weight to be stable out in Assawoman Bay, where the division is judged."

BEST OF COMPETITION

2000

TURNSTONE AND SANDPIPERS
by Larry Barth

ERNIE SPARKS

Best in World Decorative Life-size Wildfowl at the 2000 Ward World Championship.

In Their Own Words

"My original plan was to have lots of turnstones and a few purples. Scaling that down left me with a couple of turnstones and one purple, which I couldn't make work. I ended up switching to two purples and one turnstone. A ruddy turnstone is a strongly colored and patterned bird; it only takes one to get the idea across. The purples make up for their lack of boldness with greater numbers."

WHITE EGRET
by Gary Eigenberger

RICHARD MELINE, JR.

Best of Show, Professional Decorative Miniature, at the 2000 Wings over the Valley Wildlife Carving Show. Eigenberger's reddish egret won for decorative life-size at the same show.

WWW.WILDFOWL-CARVING.COM

COMPETITION 2001

As editor of WILDFOWL CARVING MAGAZINE, Cathy Hart had also overseen COMPETITION since its inception. COMPETITION 2001 saw the introduction of a new editor as Candi Tennant took over the role for both magazines after Hart moved on. One of the shows introduced to COMPETITION for some spotlight coverage from 2001 was the Wildlife Art and Carving Expo in Topsfield, Massachusetts. Like the other shows in COMPETITION 2001, it was part of the wildfowl carving "community" that Tennant touted in her debut editorial. That community is still going strong, 17 years later.

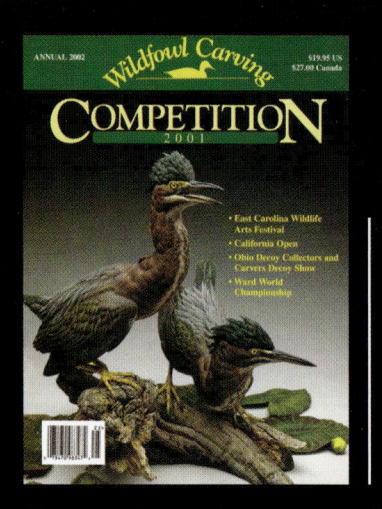

Gary Yoder carved the green herons on the cover. They won Best in Masters Decorative Life-size Wildfowl at the 2001 Ward World Championship. Ernie Sparks took the photo.

BLACK DUCKS AND HYBRID MALLARD
by Pat Godin

ERNIE SPARKS

Best in World Shootin' Rig at the 2001 Ward World Championship. Godin also won Best in World Decorative Miniature Wildfowl.

In Their Own Words

"I chose to include the hybrid with the pair of black ducks to add some freshness, uniqueness, and creativity to the rig concept. I knew there was some obvious risk in doing this bird, since there is no clear-cut standard to judge it against. Hybrids of mallards and black ducks can vary tremendously from one extreme to the other."

BROAD-WINGED HAWK
by Larry Barth

ERNIE SPARKS

Best in World Decorative Life-size Wildfowl at the 2001 Ward World Championship. This was Barth's third win in a row.

WHITE-THROATED SWIFTS
by Dan Burgette

ERNIE SPARKS

Best in World Interpretive Wood Sculpture at the 2001 Ward show. Burgette called his carving *Chasing the Next Generation*.

In Their Own Words

"The swooping grain allowed me to carve the impression of swirling air currents flowing behind the birds while still providing the strength I needed. I was able to follow the grain pattern, which preserved the strength of the piece, while carving the wood down to thin ribbons."

JAPANESE QUAIL
by Yasuko Iida

Best of Show, Decorative Life-size Non-floating, Open, at the 2001 California Open.

RICHARD MELINE, JR.

In Their Own Words

"I wanted to express the beauty of the quail's many feather layers and patterns, while also achieving a very simple, oriental feeling in the piece. . . . I studied Japanese painting as a student at the university. I strongly believe this study helped me to be creative as a carver."

GREAT BLUE HERON
by Gary Eigenberger

Best in Masters Decorative Miniature Wildfowl at the 2001 Ward World Championship.

ERNIE SPARKS

BEST OF COMPETITION

2001

DRAKE SURF SCOTER
by Lionel Dwyer

Best of Show, Floating Decorative, Open, at the 2001 Ohio Decoy Collectors and Carvers Association show. Dwyer also carved a hen that won Second Best of Show.

ERNIE SPARKS

In Their Own Words

"The surf scoter is not the most exciting species in the avian world. The drake with his monotone, yet bold, color scheme was somewhat of a challenge. I had to decide how much to carve in or paint in. The hen was fun to do with her various hues of gray and brown. She turned out to be my favorite of the two."

MALLARDS
by Richard Reeves

Best in World Floating Decorative Life-size Waterfowl Pairs at the 2001 Ward show.

ERNIE SPARKS

In Their Own Words

"The most difficult part is creating an animated carving, one not frozen in place. I try to create a pose that is different, one that makes a pleasing first impression and invites a closer inspection."

WWW.WILDFOWL-CARVING.COM

COMPETITION 2002

BOREAL OWL
by Al Jordan

ERNIE SPARKS

Best of Show, Rest of the Marsh, Open, at the 2002 Ohio Decoy Collectors and Carvers Association show. Jordan's northern pygmy owls took third.

In Their Own Words

"I was inspired by a visit from a boreal owl to Braddock Bay in the winter of 2000. These owls are rare visitors to New York. I wanted to make the carving as soft and relaxed as the real bird was in its natural surroundings."

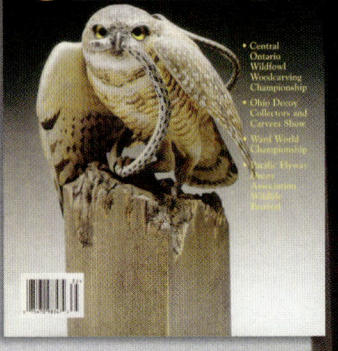

Richard Finch carved the burrowing owl on the cover. It won Best in Masters Decorative Life-size Wildfowl at the 2002 Ward World Championship. Ernie Sparks took the photo.

At the 2002 Ward World Championship, editorial assistant Dan Marsteller posed the million-dollar question to Larry Barth. Is wildfowl carving art? "There are days when that question matters, and there are days when I don't care," said Barth, who had just won his fourth consecutive best in world title in decorative life-size wildfowl. "I feel that any endeavor can be art, but nothing automatically is. In my mind the term art can be applied to anything that is executed with uncommon finesse and sensitivity." Like the editions that came before (and those that will come after), COMPETITION 2002 displayed work with plenty of finesse, and maybe some sensitivity, too.

SHOVELERS
by Tom Christie

Best in World Shootin' Rig at the 2002 Ward show. This was Christie's third win in this category.

In Their Own Words

"Using a preening position can be risky. Many times a preening bird will not project at a distance, or it may be seen by some judges as too animated."

In Their Own Words

"Whistling ducks allopreen, and I decided from day one that this was the attitude that I wanted to portray. My original intent was to have two points of contact between the birds; one at their bodies, and the second between the drake's bill and the hen's cheek."

BLACK-BELLIED WHISTLING DUCKS
by Jamie Welsh

Best in World Floating Decorative Life-size Pairs at the 2002 Ward show.

WWW.WILDFOWL-CARVING.COM

MACAWS
by Phil Galatas

Best in World Interpretive Wood Sculpture at the 2002 Ward show. Galatas titled the piece *Queen of Hearts*.

ERNIE SPARKS

In Their Own Words

"The hard part was knowing when to stop removing bulk, because I needed to maintain a certain degree of strength. With all the negative space between the leaves, the piece became very fragile."

BEST OF COMPETITION

2002

PURPLE GALLINULES
by Jason Lucio

PETER BISSET

Best of Show, Decorative Others, Open, at the 2002 Central Ontario Wildfowl Woodcarving Championship.

SANDERLINGS
by Larry Barth

ERNIE SPARKS

Best in World Decorative Life-size Wildfowl at the 2002 Ward World Championship. This was Barth's fourth straight world title in this category.

In Their Own Words

"The design was difficult because the birds are densely packed. In reality they would not touch, but for the stability of the carving, the jointery is crucial. My challenge was to make the jointery disappear. I wanted to come up with a composition that was not contrived; a casual, loose, irregular arrangement. Ultimately the goal was to make them look unarranged."

WWW.WILDFOWL-CARVING.COM

71

COMPETITION 2003

The 2003 edition of COMPETITION had something completely different—a feature by noted carver Floyd Scholz titled "The Irresistible Appeal of Sculpted Birds," that outlined some of the history of bird carving. Scholz had no doubt about the question of whether wildfowl carving was art or not. "Today's bird carvers are artists, creating in mixed media to celebrate the beauty and diversity of birds," he wrote. "Finally, bird carvings are receiving the recognition and reverence they richly deserve."

COMPETITION 2003 also included its first coverage of Winnipeg's Prairie Canada Carving Competition. The show "held the allure of unseen talent and the anticipation of a thriving competition, as I had been assured by the show chairman that I would find," noted editor Candi Derr. "And they were right."

SMEWS
by Jason Lucio

ERNIE SPARKS

Best in World Floating Decorative Life-size Pairs at the 2002 Ward World Championship.

In Their Own Words

"When researching my 1989 second best in world pairs common mergansers at an aviary, I saw my first pair of smews. Immediately I was intrigued by these regal little characters. When I saw that they were one of the four choices for this year the decision was absolute, it had to be the smews."

RED-BILLED TROPICBIRD
by Larry Barth

Best in World Decorative Life-size Wildfowl at the 2003 Ward World Championship. This was Barth's fifth consecutive world title in this category.

ERNIE SPARKS

In Their Own Words

"Red-billed Tropicbird is typical of my recent work in that it is a piece I've wanted to do for a long time. I made a very small clay model of it over ten years ago. The project stalled because I wasn't comfortable doing a bird that I had never seen. In the end, the artistic potential of the bird's dramatic form proved irresistible and I decided I shouldn't let my lack of familiarity with the subject keep me from doing a piece I felt so strongly about."

The great blue heron on the cover is by Gary Eigenberger. It won Third in World Decorative Miniature Wildfowl at the 2003 Ward World Championship. Ernie Sparks took the photo.

BARRED OWL
by Gary Eigenberger

Best of Show, Decorative Life-size Wildfowl, in the 2003 Louisiana Wildfowl Carvers Festival Gulf South Championship.

ERNIE SPARKS

In Their Own Words

"When you work with large life-size birds there is so much more energy and emotion needed to make a convincing sculpture. You're putting small details in over a much larger area. My energy was fueled by the excitement I had in my mind for the finished piece."

CALIFORNIA QUAIL
by Bob Lavender

Best of Show, Decorative Miniature Wild Birds, Open, at the 2003 Prairie Canada Carving Competition. Lavender titled the piece *California Sunshine*.

RICHARD GWIZDAK

BEST OF COMPETITION

2003

REDHEADS
by Rick Johannsen

Best in World Shootin' Rig at the 2003 Ward show.

ERNIE SPARKS

In Their Own Words

"This was my third try at the World Rig. Having carved puddle ducks for the first two tries, I wanted to carve divers. I called my friend and carving legend Cigar Daisey, for whom I have a great deal of respect, and asked his advice. Cigar said, 'You can win with redheads, two hens and a drake.' I was proud to prove him right."

DRAKE FULVOUS WHISTLING DUCK
by William Browne

Best of Show, Decorative Life-size Floating, Open, at the 2003 California Open.

RICHARD MELINE, JR.

WWW.WILDFOWL-CARVING.COM

COMPETITION 2004

One new wrinkle in the 2004 edition of COMPETITION was the inclusion of winners from the first-ever Endangered Species Contest, co-sponsored by WILDFOWL CARVING MAGAZINE and the International Wildfowl Carvers Association. Over the course of the year, IWCA-sponsored shows picked from among carvings of seven endangered species. Peter Palumbo took top honors with a Kirtland's warbler and second with a Western snowy plover. The contest joined 11 other competitions in the annual compilation of the best of the best. As managing editor Dan Marsteller noted, "the carving show is a vital part of the institution of wildfowl carving, and one that we feel should be lavishly celebrated and preserved."

DRAKE MALLARD
by Pat Godin

ERNIE SPARKS

Best of Show, Floating Decorative, Open, at the 2004 Ohio Decoy Collectors and Carvers Association show.

TREE SPARROW
by Bob Guge

Best in World Decorative Miniature Wildfowl at the 2004 Ward World Championship.

ERNIE SPARKS

In Their Own Words

"I only mounted the tree sparrow to the base shortly before the show. When I did, I discovered that the coloration of the bird and the leaves was sufficiently similar so as to camouflage the bird somewhat. I ended up adding the snow to the base so that the bird would stand out more, and it ended up working pretty well."

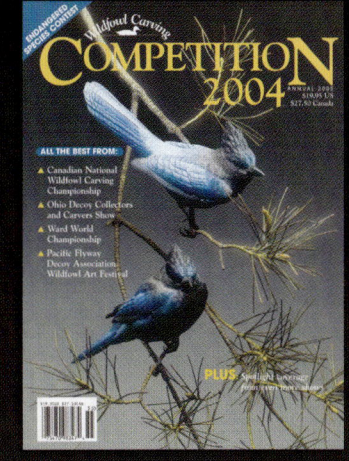

The Steller's jays on a Scotch pine on the cover are by Todd Wohlt. They won Best in World Decorative Life-size Wildfowl at the 2004 Ward World Championship. Ernie Sparks took the photo.

In Their Own Words

"The European eiders and gannet were carved from tupelo and hand-painted in oil paints. The concept for the pairing of these species was developed from my love of seabirds. Eiders and gannets are among my favorites and are fascinating species."

EIDERS AND GANNET
by Keith Mueller

Best in World Shootin' Rig at the 2004 Ward show.

ERNIE SPARKS

WIGEONS
by Richard Reeves

Best of Show in the Gulf South Championship at the 2004 Louisiana Wildfowl Carvers Festival.

KEN MAGEE

BEST OF COMPETITION

2004

YELLOWLEGS
by Tommy Stewart

Best in Show, Gunning Shorebirds, Open, at the 2004 ODCCA show.

ERNIE SPARKS

In Their Own Words

"I studied this bird through its migration period, taking as many notes and preliminary sketches as I could before it moved on. Taking my time starting in clay, then turning to wood, made the difference in the success of its final form."

YELLOW WARBLER
by Bruce Lepper

Best of Show, Decorative Songbirds B, Open, at the 2004 Canadian National Wildfowl Carving Championship.

PETER BISSET

In Their Own Words

"The yellowing leaves of the serviceberry were designed to complement the bird by reflecting its coloration and markings, thereby unifying the composition."

WWW.WILDFOWL-CARVING.COM

COMPETITION 2005

In his introduction to COMPETITION 2005, new editor Bill Einsig pondered what the publication's offer to present "all the best" really meant. Obviously, there are some wonderful carvers who never enter competitions, and the winning work at some shows is better than that at others. The role of COMPETITION is to show the best from each show. "Each year we're amazed at the talent and creativity of carvers who stretch the envelope of wildfowl carving, try new approaches, and communicate a message so clearly," wrote Einsig.

FERRUGINOUS HAWK
by Jeff Krete

ERNIE SPARKS

Best in Masters Decorative Miniature Wildfowl at the 2005 Ward World Championship.

Peter Kaune carved the piping plover on the cover. It won the Endangered Species Championship in 2005 and also took Second Best of Show at the California Open. Bill Einsig took the photo.

MALLARDS
by Thomas Cornicelli

ERNIE SPARKS

First in Gunning Pairs at the 2005 Ward show.

REDHEADS
by Dick Rhode

ERNIE SPARKS

Best in World Shootin' Rig at the 2005 Ward show.

In Their Own Words

"The three-bird rig creates a great challenge because you want the birds to look good up close for indoor viewing, although they must project very strongly from a distance, all the while complementing one another. . . . I wanted the birds to exhibit powerful redhead characteristics when viewed from any angle."

WWW.WILDFOWL-CARVING.COM

INDIGO BUNTINGS
by Larry Barth

Best in World Decorative Life-size Wildfowl at the 2005 Ward show.

ERNIE SPARKS

BARRED OWL
by Floyd Scholz

First in Master's Decorative Life-size Wildfowl at the 2005 Ward show.

ERNIE SPARKS

BEST OF COMPETITION

QUETZAL
by Keith Mueller

Best in World Decorative Miniature Wildfowl at the 2005 Ward show.

ERNIE SPARKS

COMPETITION 2006

COMPETITION 2006 was just packed with shows—a dozen in all, plus results of the various contests sponsored by the International Wildfowl Carvers Association. And, as editor Bill Einsig pointed out, "Each show has a distinctive flavor that stems from the sponsoring club, the history of the show, and the surrounding culture." Just as there is a great diversity in the carvings, there is a great variety in the shows, whether it's the Ward World Championship in Maryland or the Columbia Flyway competition in Vancouver, Washington.

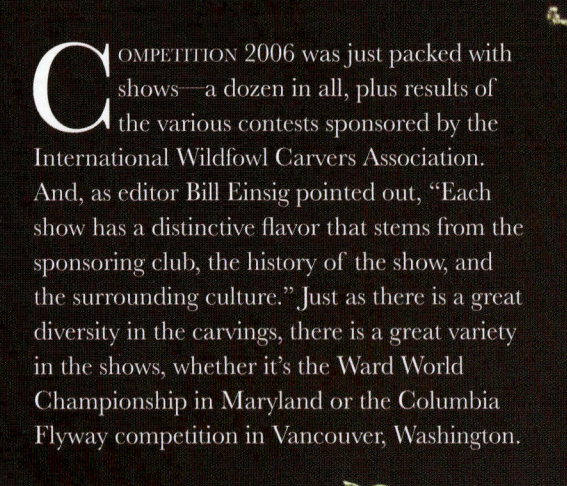

'I'WIS AND OHEA LEHUA
by Larry Barth

Best in World Decorative Life-size Wildfowl at the 2006 Ward World Championship.

THE WARD MUSEUM

The pintail on the cover is by Marcus Schultz. It won Second in World Decorative Life-size Wildfowl at the 2006 Ward World Championship. Schultz provided the photo.

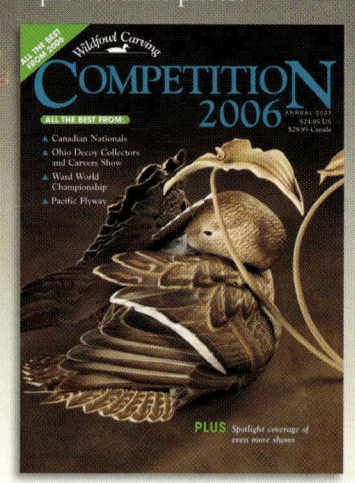

BARN SWALLOWS
by John Leeder

ROY BARKHOUSE

Best of Show at the 2006 Canadian National Wildfowl Carving Championship.

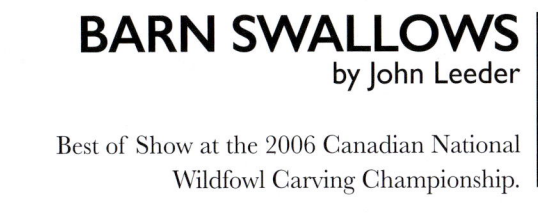

In Their Own Words

"I believe good art should stir an emotion, tell a story, or reflect on a memory. I want my sculptures to be slightly outside the box. I hope those who view my work see more than a perfect bird."

AMERICAN KESTREL
by Gilles Prud'homme

ROY BARKHOUSE

First, Decorative Birds of Prey, Open, at the 2006 Canadian National Wildfowl Carving Championship.

WWW.WILDFOWL-CARVING.COM

85

SECRETARY BIRD
by Gary Eigenberger

Best in World Decorative Miniature Wildfowl at the 2006 Ward show.

THE WARD MUSEUM

86

BEST OF COMPETITION

2006

ANTIQUE MERGANSER
by R.D. Wilson

Best of Ducks, Doubtful Antiques, at the 2006 Pacific Flyway show.

ROB SOLARI

HEN PINTAIL
by Pat Godin

Best of Show, Decorative Floating Waterfowl, Open, at the 2006 Ohio Decoy Collectors and Carvers Association show. The pintail also won Best in Masters Floating Decorative Waterfowl at the Ward show.

PAT GODIN

COMPETITION 2007

New editor Tom Huntington was impressed by the "Wow" factor he felt at carving shows. "As good as the birds look in print, the best way to experience them is by visiting the shows and seeing the work up close and personal," he wrote. However, the birds in print did look pretty good, too, and the carvings in the 2007 edition represented the wide variety of work that people had come to expect from COMPETITION over the past 20 years. According to Huntington, "all of them demonstrate the strange alchemy that allows talented artists to create seeming life from inanimate wood. It's quite a feat."

PLATE-BILLED MOUNTAIN TOUCAN
by Tom Horn

Best in World Decorative Life-size Wildfowl at the 2007 Ward World Championship.

COURTESY THE WARD MUSEUM, BY WES DEMAREST

In Their Own Words

"I was trying to get more than just a bird sitting there.... I thought it would be competitive, but I didn't know I'd win.... It can be intimidating, competing with people who have 20 or 30 years' experience."

NUTHATCH
by Alan Bell

Best of Show, Open, at the 2007 Canadian National Wildfowl Carving Championship.

ROY BARKHOUSE

David Inglefield carved the endangered St. Vincent parrot on the cover. It won Best in Advanced Decorative Life-size Wildfowl at the 2007 Ward World Championship. Wes Demarest took the photo for the Ward Museum.

DRAKE MALLARD
by Jean Minaudier

People's Choice at the 2007 Ward show. Minaudier called the sculpture *Suzie and the Sweet 16*.

COURTESY THE WARD MUSEUM, BY WES DEMAREST

BEST OF COMPETITION

2007

FOX SPARROW
by Peter Kaune

Best of Show, Decorative Life-size Non-floating, Open, at the 2007 California Open.

BILL EINSIG

DRAKE PINTAIL
by Pat Godin

Best in Show, Life-size Floating Decorative, Open, at the 2007 Ohio Decoy Collectors and Carvers Association show.

COURTESY THE WARD MUSEUM, BY WES DEMAREST

2008–2017

During the last decade, COMPETITION has continued to showcase the "best of the best." Some shows have closed their doors—the East Carolina Wildlife Arts Festival had its last carving competition in 2016, and the California Open ended after the 2017 show. We also lost the Wings 'n' Water Festival, and the Northeast Waterfowl Festival made a couple of appearances before it, too, faded away. On the plus side, the Louisiana Wildfowl Carvers and Collectors Guild Festival returned to our pages in COMPETITION 2011, the show's third outing since Hurricane Katrina forced a temporary hiatus in 2005. COMPETITION started coverage of the Quinte Woodcarvers Competition in 2012. In general, though, the show lineup has remained fairly consistent, while the work we've covered has remained consistently superb. That's a tradition COMPETITION plans to continue for the next three decades and beyond.

SAW-WHET OWL
by Jerry Simchuk

First in Open, Best of Division, Best of Show, Sunday's People's Choice, and the Mayor's Award at the 2008 Columbia Flyway show.

MATT FURCRON

SHORBIRDS
by Bob Berry

First (European dotterel), Second (godwit), and Third (stilt sandpiper), Decorative Smoothie Shorebirds and Wading Birds at the 2008 Ward World Championship. The sandpiper also won Best of Show, Gunning Shorebirds, Open, at the Ohio Decoy Collectors and Carvers show.

COURTESY THE WARD MUSEUM, BY WES DEMAREST

In Their Own Words

"There are some people who are fast—and I'm fast—but I'm always trying to police myself. I don't want to hurt the piece and the quality. . . . I'm not devastated if I don't win, as I've demonstrated with hundreds and hundreds of losses over the years. But I keep trying."

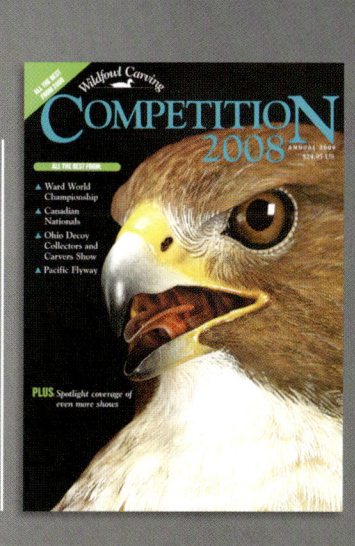

Floyd Scholz carved the red-tailed hawk that appeared on the COMPETITION 2008 cover. It won People's Choice at the 2008 Ward World Championship. Photo courtesy the Ward Museum, by Wes Demarest.

EARED GREBES
by Todd Wohlt

Best in World Decorative Life-size Wildfowl at the 2008 Ward World Championship. Wohlt also won Best in World Decorative Miniature Wildfowl that year.

COURTESY THE WARD MUSEUM, BY WES DEMAREST

MERGANSERS AND LOON
by Rich Smoker

Best in World Shootin' Rig at the 2008 Ward show.

COURTESY THE WARD MUSEUM, BY WES DEMAREST

2008

MACAW
by Victor Paroyan

Best of Show at the 2008 Canadian National Wildfowl Carving Championship.

INTERPRETIVE WREN
by Byrn and Joanne Watson

First in Open and Best in Division at the 2008 Columbia Flyway Wildlife Show.

KILLDEER
by Larry Barth

Best in World Decorative Life-size Wildfowl at the 2009 Ward World Championship.

COURTESY THE WARD MUSEUM, BY WES DEMAREST

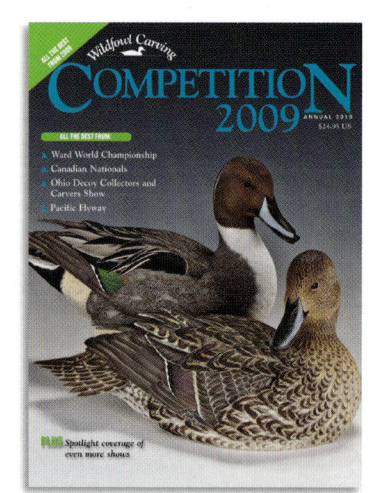

Pat Godin carved the pintails on the COMPETITION 2009 cover. They won Best in World Floating Decorative Life-size Waterfowl Pairs at the 2009 Ward World Championship. It was the second year in a row that Godin won the world pairs division. Photo by Wes Demarest, courtesy the Ward Museum.

DRAKE CINNAMON TEAL
by Mark Strucko

Best in Show, Decorative Life-size Floating, Open, at the 2009 East Carolina Wildlife Arts Festival. Strucko also took second with a black duck.

BILL EINSIG

BEST OF COMPETITION

2009

NORTHERN WATER THRUSHES
by Josh Guge

Best of Show, Decorative Life-size Non-floating, Open, at the 2009 California Open.

ELSA FLORES

SHARP-SHINNED HAWK AND BLUEBIRD
by Gary Eigenberger

Best in World Decorative Miniature Wildfowl at the 2009 Ward show.

COURTESY THE WARD MUSEUM, BY WES DEMAREST

WWW.WILDFOWL-CARVING.COM

ROSE-BREASTED GROSBEAK
by Bruce Lepper

Best in World Decorative Life-size Wildfowl at the 2010 Ward World Championship.

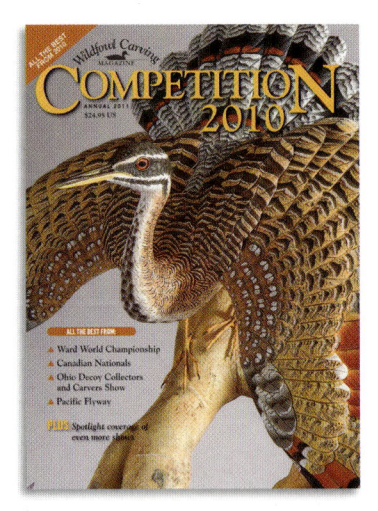

Roy Barkhouse photographed Gilles Prud'homme's sunbittern, which won the Al Forler Best of Show Award at the 2010 Canadian National Wildfowl Carving Championship.

COURTESY THE WARD MUSEUM, BY WES DEMAREST

INDIAN BLUE PEACOCK
by Daniel Montano

Best in Show, Palm Fronds, at the 2010 California Open.

ELSA FLORES

98   BEST OF COMPETITION

2011

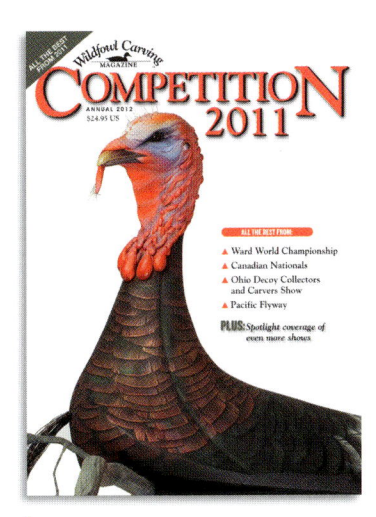

Daniel Montano's colorful turkey won the decorative palm frond competition at the 2011 California Open. Elsa Flores took the photo.

BLACKBURNIAN WARBLER
by Lana Cowell

Best of Show, Open, at the 2011 Prairie Canada Carving Championship.

RICHARD GWIZDAK

YELLOW-RUMPED WARBLER
by Larry Barth

Best in World Decorative Life-size Wildfowl at the 2011 Ward show.

COURTESY THE WARD MUSEUM, BY WES DEMAREST

WWW.WILDFOWL-CARVING.COM

LONG-TAILED DUCKS
by Thomas Flemming

Best in World Shootin' Rig (Jimmy Vizier Memorial Award) at the 2011 Ward show.

COURTESY THE WARD MUSEUM, BY WES DEMAREST

GREAT BLUE HERONS
by Ashley Gray

Second Best in World Interpretive Sculpture and People's Choice at the 2011 Ward World Championship. Gray called the sculpture *Hannah's Setting Sun*.

COURTESY THE WARD MUSEUM, BY WES DEMAREST

BEST OF COMPETITION

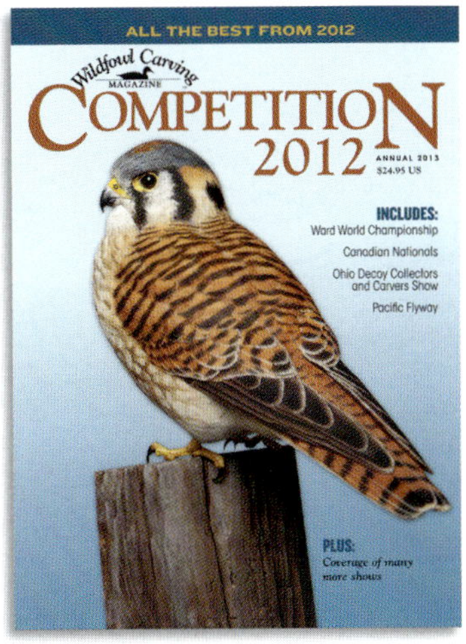

2012

An American kestrel by Bruce Lepper appeared on the 2013 edition's cover. It won the M&T Printing Group purchase award at the 2013 Canadian National Wildfowl Carving Championship. Roy Barkhouse took the photo.

AMERICAN AVOCET
by Gary De Cew

Best of Show, Soon-to-be-Antiques, at the 2012 California Open.

In Their Own Words

"We need to promote the use of our hands and hand tools. Hand-made art pieces that are made one at a time are unique and imperfect. That's what makes them beautiful!"

ELSA FLORES

PINK-HEADED DUCKS
by Jeff Krete

Best of Show and Best of Class, Open, at the 2012 Canadian National Wildfowl Carving Championship.

ROY BARKHOUSE

WWW.WILDFOWL-CARVING.COM

101

VIOLET SABREWING HUMMINGBIRDS
by Thomas Horn

Best in World Decorative Life-size Wildfowl at the 2012 Ward World Championship.

COURTESY THE WARD MUSEUM, BY BILL EINSIG

BEST OF COMPETITION

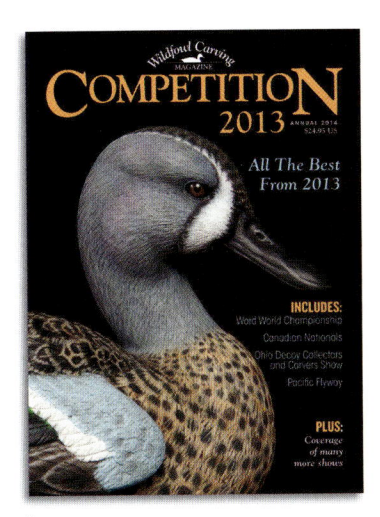

2013

POTOO
by Keith Mueller

Best in World Decorative Life-size Wildfowl at the 2013 Ward World Championship.

COURTESY THE WARD MUSEUM, BY BILL EINSIG

Gary Brocklebank won a blue ribbon at the 2013 Canadian National Wildfowl Carving Championship with the blue-winged teal that appeared on the cover. Roy Barkhouse took the photo.

DRAKE SCAUP, HEN RED-BREASTED MERGANSER, AND HEN MALLARD
by Ben Heinemann and Walter Gaskill

First (Gaskill scaup), Second (Heinemann mallard), and third (Heinemann merganser) Best of Show, IWCA-style Decoys, at the Core Sound Decoy Festival.

BILL EINSIG

WWW.WILDFOWL-CARVING.COM

NORTHERN HAWK OWL
by Tom Baldwin

First, M&T Printing Group Purchase Award, at the 2013 Canadian National Wildfowl Carving Championship.

ROY BARKHOUSE

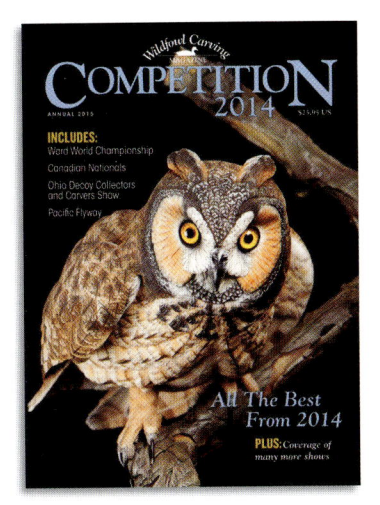

2014

CAROLINA WREN
by Larry Barth

Best in World Decorative Life-size Wildfowl at the 2014 Ward World Championship.

COURTESY THE WARD MUSEUM, BY BILL EINSIG

Al Jordan carved the long-eared owl that appeared on the cover. It won Best in Show, Open Decorative Life-size Non-floating, at the 2014 East Carolina Wildlife Arts Festival. Sherri Taylor took the photo.

DRAKE MALLARD
by Mike Bonner

Best in Gulf South Charles Frank Decorative Decoy at the 2014 Louisiana Wildfowl Carvers and Collectors Guild show.

RICHARD REEVES

WWW.WILDFOWL-CARVING.COM

PINE GROSBEAK
by Harvey Welch

Razertip Industries Purchase Award at the 2014 Prairie Canada Carving Championship. Welch also won First and Second Best of Show, Open.

RICHARD GWIZDAK

HEN REDHEAD
by Jack Cox

Best of Show, IWCA-style Decoys, at the 2014 Core Sound Decoy Festival.

BILL EINSIG

2015

Gary Eigenberger's brown thrashers won Best in Master's Decorative Life-size Wildfowl at the 2015 Ward World Championship. Alan Wycheck took the photo for the Ward Museum.

GREAT HORNED OWL
by Al Jordan

Best of Show, Decorative Life-size Wildfowl, Professional, at the 2015 East Carolina Wildlife Festival.

BRENT HOOD

DRAKE WESTERN GREBE
by Ted Smith

Best of Show and Best of Division, Open, at the 2015 Columbia Flyway Wildlife Show.

MATT FURCRON

WWW.WILDFOWL-CARVING.COM

APLOMADO FALCON
by Del Herbert

Best in Show, Palm Frond Decorative Raptors, at the 2015 California Open.

ELSA FLORES

BOHEMIAN WAXWINGS
by Larry Barth

Best in World Decorative Life-size Wildfowl at the 2015 Ward World Championship.

COURTESY THE WARD MUSEUM, BY ALAN WYCHECK

BEST OF COMPETITION

2016

Todd Wohlt carved the anhinga on the cover. It won Second Best in World Decorative Miniature Wildfowl at the 2016 Ward World Championship. Photograph courtesy of the Ward Museum, by Alan Wycheck.

DRAKE CINNAMON TEAL
by Bunny Farley

Best in Show, Decorative Life-size Non-floating, Open, at the 2016 California Open.

ELSA FLORES

LIVINGSTONE'S TURACO
by Thomas Horn

Best in World Decorative Life-size Wildfowl at the 2016 Ward show.

COURTESY THE WARD MUSEUM, BY ALAN WYCHECK

WWW.WILDFOWL-CARVING.COM

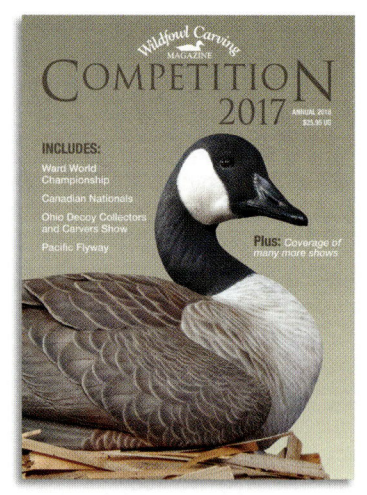

DRAKE WIGEON
by Brad Snodgrass

First, Decorative Life-size Floating, Open, at the 2017 Pacific Flyway Decoy Classic.

In Their Own Words

"What a lot of people don't understand about the airbrush is that it's not as much about the airbrush as it is about the stenciling. It's about the negative space that you leave, as opposed to where the paint goes. And then the ability to move on and disguise that with a real brush."

Wayne Simkin carved the Canada goose on the cover. It won Best in Show and First in Canadian Master Class at the 2017 Canadian National Wildfowl Carving Championship. Roy Barkhouse took the photo.

ROB SOLARI

CAPE SUGARBIRDS
by Gerald Painter

Best in World Decorative Miniature Wildfowl at the 2017 Ward World Championship.

COURTESY THE WARD MUSEUM, BY ALAN WYCHECK

BEST OF COMPETITION

REDDISH EGRET
by Gary Eigenberger

Best in World Decorative Life-size Wildfowl at the 2017 Ward show.

COURTESY THE WARD MUSEUM, BY ALAN WYCHECK

Blue Ribbon BASES

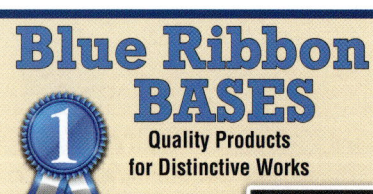

Quality Products for Distinctive Works

92 Sylmar Road
Rising Sun, MD 21911
(410) 658-1474
E-mail:
blueribbonbases@aol.com
blueribbonbases.net

CATALOG AVAILABLE ONLINE

KV Woodcarving Supplies

For All Your Carving Needs

Largest Selection of Carving Supplies in Eastern Canada

Noted for fast and friendly service
(506) 847-3052 • Fax: (506) 849-3052

Email: kvwcs@nbnet.nb.ca
www.kvwoodcarvingsupplies.com

AD INDEX

Blue Ribbon Bases	112
Core Sound Decoy Festival	3
Dux' Decoys	112
Fox Chapel Publishing	Inside Back Cover
Hummul Carving Company	Inside Front Cover, 1
International Wildfowl Carvers Association (IWCA)	3
The Jaymes Co	112
Krausman's Woodcarving Studio	112
KV Woodcarving	112
RazerTip Industries, Inc.	4, Back Cover
WCM Book Club	13
WCM Subscriptions	3

Krausman's Wildlife Reference Photos & Woodcarving Studio

REFERENCE PHOTOS | CARVING SEMINARS | SUPPLIES

Jim Krausman & Pamyla L Krausman

www.referencephotos.com
1-877-KRAUSMA
jmkrausman@gmail.com
Gwinn, Michigan

MISSING AN ISSUE? WE CAN HELP!

Order back issues of WILDFOWL CARVING MAGAZINE and COMPETITION from

www.wildfowl-carving.com.

Or call (toll-free)
(877) 762-8034 (US)
(866) 375-7257 (Canada)

Dux' Dekes Decoy Company

Since 1987, producing the finest carving blanks on the market today. Ducks, geese, loons, shorebirds, songbirds, raptors, upland game, wading birds and gunners. We are now offering tupelo in our Premire blanks, along with select shorebirds, uplands gamebirds, songbirds and raptors. You'll not find a wider, more diverse, high quality selection of blanks anywhere.

Kingfisher, BBL17, 11 inch, available in pine and tupelo

800-553-4725
www.duxdekes.com
1356 North Rd.
Greenwich, New York, 12834

Jaymes Company

Where Service and Knowledge Make a Difference!

Specializing in Woodcarving Tools and Supplies

Keith Mueller's Studio

More Than 4,000 Items in Stock

Visit us on the web:
www.jaymescompany.com

Or Call Toll Free (888) 638-8998

Forest Hill, MD

Supplying Carvers for 41 Years